50
MODERN
AMERICAN
& BRITISH
POETS,
1920-1970

Books by Louis Untermeyer

The Pursuit of Poetry
A Treasury of Great Humor
Lives of the Poets
The Letters of Robert Frost to Louis Untermeyer
Modern American Poetry
Modern British Poetry
Cat O' Nine Tales
50 Modern American & British Poets, 1920–1970

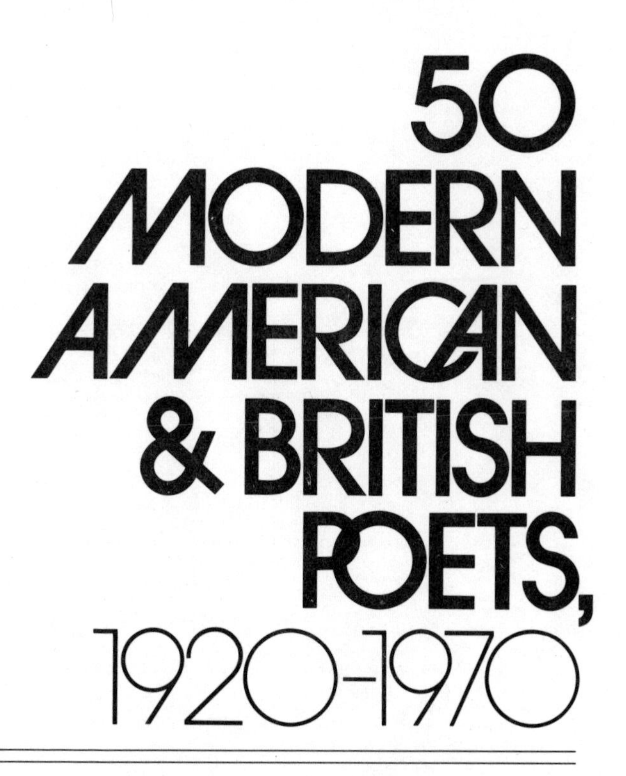

Edited, with a Biographical
and Critical Commentary, by

LOUIS UNTERMEYER

DAVID McKAY COMPANY, INC.
New York

50 MODERN AMERICAN & BRITISH POETS
1920–1970

LIBRARY OF CONGRESS CATALOG CARD NUMBER: 72-89118
MANUFACTURED IN THE UNITED STATES OF AMERICA
Designed by Bob Antler

ACKNOWLEDGMENTS

The editor and publisher have made every effort to trace the ownership of all copyright material and to secure permission from the holders of the copyright. In the event of any question arising as to the use of any selection, the publisher and editor, while expressing regret for any inadvertent error, will be glad to make the necessary correction in future printings.

The editor and publisher gratefully acknowledge permission to reprint the following poems and express their thanks to the following individuals and publishers:

To John Malcolm Brinnin for "Nuns at Eve" and "Grave Mind I Love."

To Random House for:

"Musée des Beaux Arts," "The Unknown Citizen," "In Memory of W. B. Yeats," copyright 1940 and renewed 1968 by W. H. Auden. Reprinted from *Collected Shorter Poems 1927–1957* by W. H. Auden, by permission of Random House, Inc.

"An elementary school classroom," copyright 1942 and renewed 1970 by Stephen Spender. Reprinted from *Selected Poems* by Stephen Spender, by permission of Random House, Inc.

"I think continually of those," copyright 1934 and renewed 1962 by Stephen Spender. Reprinted from *Selected Poems* by Stephen Spender, by permission of Random House, Inc.

To Alfred A. Knopf, Inc. for:

"April Inventory," copyright © 1957 by W. D. Snodgrass. Reprinted from *Heart's Needle,* by W. D. Snodgrass, by permission of Alfred A. Knopf, Inc.

"Peter Quince at the Clavier," copyright 1932 and renewed 1951 by Wallace Stevens. Reprinted from *The Collected Poems of Wallace Stevens,* by permission of Alfred A. Knopf, Inc.

"The Poems of Our Climate" and "Of Modern Poetry," copyright 1942 by Wallace Stevens and renewed 1970 by Holly Stevens Stephenson. Reprinted from *The Collected Poems of Wallace Stevens*, by permission of Alfred A. Knopf, Inc.

To Harold Matson Company, Inc. for:

"An Elementary Classroom in a Slum, copyright © 1942 by Stephen Spender. Copyright renewed 1970 by the author. "I Think Continually of Those Who Were Truly Great," copyright © 1934 by Stephen Spender. Copyright renewed 1962 by the author. Reprinted by permission of Harold Matson Company, Inc.

To The Macmillan Company for:

"Nevertheless," "The Wood-Weasel," and "The Mind Is an Enchanting Thing." Reprinted with permission of The Macmillan Company from *Collected Poems* by Marianne Moore. Copyright 1944 by Marianne Moore, renewed 1972 by Marianne Moore.

To Atheneum Publishers, Inc. for:

"Samuel Sewall," from *The Hard Hours* by Anthony Hecht. Copyright © 1954 by Anthony E. Hecht. Reprinted by permission of Atheneum Publishers.

"Homework" from *To See, To Take* by Mona Van Duyn. Copyright © 1969 by Mona Van Duyn. Reprinted by permission of Atheneum Publishers. Appeared originally in *Poetry.*

"Western Country" from *The Carrier of Ladders* by W. S. Merwin. Copyright © 1970 by W. S. Merwin. Reprinted by permission of Atheneum Publishers. Appeared originally in *Harper's Bazaar.*

"More Light! More Light!" and "It Out-Herods Herod. Pray You, Avoid It." from *The Hard Hours* by Anthony Hecht. Copyright © 1961, 1966 by Anthony E. Hecht. Reprinted by permission of Atheneum Publishers. "More Light! More Light!" appeared originally in *Hudson Review.* "It Out-Herods Herod. Pray You, Avoid It." appeared originally in *Kenyon Review.*

"The Woman At The Washington Zoo" from *The Woman at the Washington Zoo* by Randall Jarrell. Copyright © 1960 by Randall Jarrell. Reprinted by permission of Atheneum Publishers.

To Farrar, Straus & Giroux, Inc. for:

"The Prodigal," "Florida," and "The Armadillo" from *The Complete Poems* by Elizabeth Bishop.

"Life, Friends, Is Boring" from *Dream Songs* by John Berryman.
"Today Is It? Is It Today?" from *Sonnets by John Berryman* by John Berryman.
"A Letter from Brooklyn" and "Coral" from *Selected Poems by Derek Walcott* by Derek Walcott.
"For the Union Dead" from *For the Union Dead* by Robert Lowell.
"Man and Wife" and "Skunk Hour" from *Life Studies* by Robert Lowell. Reprinted with the permission of Farrar, Straus & Giroux, Inc. from *For the Union Dead* by Robert Lowell, copyright © 1960 by Robert Lowell. From *Life Studies* by Robert Lowell, copyright © 1958 by Robert Lowell. From *Selected Poems* by Derek Walcott, copyright © 1962, 1964 by Derek Walcott. From *77 Dream Songs* by John Berryman, copyright © 1959, 1962, 1963, 1964 by John Berryman. From *Berryman's Sonnets*, copyright © 1952, 1967 by John Berryman. From *The Complete Poems* by Elizabeth Bishop, copyright © 1939, 1951, 1957, 1969 by Elizabeth Bishop. "90 North" and "The Death of the Ball Turret Gunner" from *Selected Poems* by Randall Jarrell. Reprinted with the permission of Farrar, Straus & Giroux, Inc. from *The Complete Poems* by Randall Jarrell, copyright © 1941, 1945, 1969 by Mrs. Randall Jarrell, copyright renewed 1968 by Mrs. Randall Jarrell.

For personal permission to reprint, the editor and publisher are grateful to:

John Malcolm Brinnin for "The Ascension: 1925," from *The Selected Poems of John Malcolm Brinnin.*

Richard Eberhart for "Man and Nature," originally published in *Saturday Review.*

James G. Hepburn and Chatto & Windus Ltd. for "The Fired Pot," "Self-Analysis," "A Love Letter," and "Meditation at Kew," from *Selected Poems by Anna Wickham.*

Erica Jong for "The Eggplant Epithalamion."

Greg Kuzma for "Poetry" which originally appeared in *Poetry: A Magazine of Verse.*

Monica McCall, IFA, for "Effort at Speech Between Two People," from *Theory of Flight*, copyright © 1935 by Yale University, copyright © 1960 by Muriel Rukeyser; "Boy With His Hair Cut Short," from *Water-lily Fire*, copyright © 1962 by Muriel Rukeyser; "Bringing," from *Greenflag* (City Lights Books) copyright © 1969 by Muriel Rukeyser.

Louis Simpson for "Mashkin Hill," which originally appeared in the London *Times Literary Supplement.*

Anne Sexton for "Angel of Clean Sheets," which originally appeared in *The New Republic.*

May Swenson for "The Thickening Mat," which originally appeared in *The New York Times.*

Richard Wilbur for "The Writer," which originally appeared in *The New Republic.*

Adrienne Rich for "Living in Sin," from *The Diamond Cutters* published by Harper & Row, New York, 1955.

To Faber and Faber Ltd. for:

"Musée des Beaux Arts," "The Unknown Citizen," and "In Memory of W. B. Yeats," by W. H. Auden. Reprinted by permission of Faber and Faber Ltd. From *Collected Shorter Poems 1927–1957.*

"Her Husband" and "Pibroch" by Ted Hughes. Reprinted by permission of Faber and Faber Ltd. From *Wodwo.*

To David Higham Associates, Ltd. for:

"The Drunk in the Furnace" and "Small Woman on Swallow Street," from *The Drunk in the Furnace* by W. S. Merwin, published by Rupert Hart-Davis.

To W. W. Norton & Company, Inc. for:

"Planetarium," reprinted from *The Will to Change,* Poems, 1968–1970 by Adrienne Rich. Copyright © 1971 by W. W. Norton & Company, Inc. Reprinted by permission of W. W. Norton & Company, Inc.

To City Light Books for:

"A Supermarket in California" from *Howl and Other Poems* by Allen Ginsberg. Copyright © 1956, 1959 by Allen Ginsberg. Reprinted by permission of City Light Books.

"Kaddish" from *Kaddish and Other Poems* by Allen Ginsberg. Copyright © 1961 by Allen Ginsberg. Reprinted by permission of City Light Books.

To Harold Ober Associates for:

"The Drunk in the Furnace" and "Small Woman on Swallow Street" from *The Drunk in the Furnace* by W. S. Merwin. Copyright © 1957, 1958 by W. S. Merwin. Reprinted by permission of Harold Ober Associates, Inc.

To Delacorte Press for:

"Rear Vision," copyright © 1954 by William Jay Smith, and "Hull Bay,

St. Thomas," copyright © 1970 by William Jay Smith; from *New And Selected Poems* by William Jay Smith. A Seymour Lawrence Book/Delacorte Press. Reprinted by permission of the publisher. Originally appeared in *The New Yorker.*

"Skin Diving in the Virgins," copyright © 1964 by The New Yorker Magazine, Inc. From *Skin Diving in the Virgins and Other Poems* by John Malcolm Brinnin. A Seymour Lawrence Book/Delacorte Press. Reprinted by permission of the publisher.

To Holt, Rinehart and Winston, Inc. for:

"Mending Wall," "The Silken Tent" and "Directive" from *The Poetry of Robert Frost* edited by Edward Connery Lathem. Copyright 1930, 1939, 1947, © 1969 by Holt, Rinehart and Winston, Inc. Copyright 1942, © 1958 by Robert Frost. Copyright © 1967, 1970 by Lesley Frost Ballantine. Reprinted by permission of Holt, Rinehart and Winston, Inc.

"The Quarrel" and "The Teacher" from *Fruits and Vegetables* by Erica Jong. Copyright © 1968, 1970, 1971 by Erica Mann Jong. Reprinted by permission of Holt, Rinehart and Winston, Inc.

"The Quarrel" and "The Teacher" from *Fruits and Vegetables* by Erica Jong. Reprinted by permission of International Famous Agency. Copyright © 1971 by Erica Mann Jong.

To The International Famous Agency for:

"Some Trees" and "The Painter" from *Some Trees* by John Ashbery. Reprinted by permission of International Famous Agency. Copyright © 1956 by John Ashbery.

To The Viking Press, Inc. for:

"Moschus Moschiferus." From *New Poems* by A. D. Hope. Copyright © 1969 by A. D. Hope. Reprinted by permission of The Viking Press, Inc.
"The Brides." From *Collected Poems 1930–1965* by A. D. Hope. Copyright © 1963, 1966 in all countries of the International Copyright Union by A. D. Hope. All rights reserved. Reprinted by permission of The Viking Press, Inc.
"Imperial Adam." From *Collected Poems 1930–1965* by A. D. Hope. Copyright © 1963, 1966 in all countries of the International Copyright Union by A. D. Hope. All rights reserved. Reprinted by permission of The Viking Press, Inc.

To Chatto and Windus Ltd. for:

"The Groundhog" and "If I could only live at the pitch that is near madness" from *Collected Poems 1930–1960* by Richard Eberhart. Reprinted by permission of Chatto and Windus Ltd.

To Oxford University Press, Inc. for:
"The Groundhog" and "If I could only live. . . ." From *Collected Poems* 1930–1960 by Richard Eberhart. Copyright © 1960 by Richard Eberhart. Reprinted by permission of Oxford University Press, Inc.
"A Letter from the Grass" and "The Census-Takers." From *Collected Poems* by Conrad Aiken. Copyright © 1953, 1970 by Conrad Aiken. Reprinted by permission of Oxford University Press, Inc.

To Liveright Publishing Corporation for:
"Voyages II" and "The Broken Tower" from *The Complete Poems and Selected Letters and Prose of Hart Crane* by Hart Crane. Permission of Liveright, Publishers, New York. Copyright © 1933, 1958, 1966 by Liveright Publishing Corporation.

To Little, Brown and Company for:
"The Portrait." Copyright © 1971 by Stanley Kunitz. From *The Testing Tree* by Stanley Kunitz, by permission of Atlantic-Little, Brown and Co.
"The War Against the Trees." Copyright © 1957, by Stanley Kunitz. From *Selected Poems* 1928–1958 by Stanley Kunitz, by permission of Atlantic-Little, Brown and Co.

To Corinth Books, Inc. for:
"For Hettie" from *Preface to a Twenty Volume Suicide Note* by Le Roi Jones. Copyright © 1961 by Le Roi Jones. Reprinted by permission of Corinth Books.

To Harcourt Brace Jovanovich, Inc. for:
"The Hollow Men," "Journey of the Magi" and "The Word of the Lord." From *Collected Poems 1909–1962* by T. S. Eliot copyright, © 1936 by Harcourt Brace Jovanovich, Inc., copyright © 1963, 1964, by T. S. Eliot. Reprinted by permission of the publisher.
"my father moved through dooms of love." Copyright 1940 by E. E. Cummings; copyright © 1968 by Marion Morehouse Cummings. Reprinted from *Poems 1923–1954* by E. E. Cummings by permission of Harcourt Brace Jovanovich, Inc.
"Now that, more nearest even than your fate." Copyright © 1962 by E. E. Cummings. Reprinted from his volume *73 Poems* by permission of Harcourt Brace Jovanovich, Inc.
"Advice to a prophet." Copyright © 1959 by Richard Wilbur. Reprinted from his volume *Advice to a Prophet and Other Poems* by permission of Harcourt Brace Jovanovich, Inc. First published in *The New Yorker*. "Digging for China." From *Things of This World*, © 1956 by Richard Wilbur. Reprinted by permission of Harcourt Brace Jovanovich, Inc.

"Things" and "After Midnight." Copyright © 1965 by Louis Simpson. Reprinted from his volume *Selected Poems* by permission of Harcourt Brace Jovanovich, Inc. First published in *The New Yorker.*

"My Great-Grandfather's Slaves." © 1965 by Wendell Berry. Reprinted from his volume *Openings* by permission of Harcourt Brace Jovanovich, Inc.

"Dark with Power." From *Openings*, © 1968, by Wendell Berry. Reprinted by permission of Harcourt Brace Jovanovich, Inc.

To Olwyn Hughes for:

"Morning Song," "The Applicant" and "Daddy" from *Ariel* by Sylvia Plath. Published by Faber & Faber, copyright © 1965 by Ted Hughes. Reprinted by permission of Olwyn Hughes.

To Harper and Row, Publishers, Inc. for:

From *Ariel* by Sylvia Plath: "Morning Song." Copyright © 1961 by Ted Hughes. "The Applicant" and "Daddy." Copyright © 1963 by Ted Hughes. By permission of Harper & Row, Publishers, Inc.

From *Wodwo* by Ted Hughes: "Her Husband" and "Pibroch." Copyright © 1961 by Ted Hughes. By permission of Harper & Row, Publishers, Inc.

From *After Experience* by W. D. Snodgrass: "Mementos I." Copyright © 1960 by W. D. Snodgrass. "What We Said." Copyright © 1958 by W. D. Snodgrass. By permission of Harper & Row Publishers, Inc.

From *The World of Gwendolyn Brooks* (1971): "We Real Cool." Copyright © 1959 by Gwendolyn Brooks. "the rites for Cousin Vit." Copyright 1949 by Gwendolyn Brooks Blakely. "manicure" from *Beauty Shoppe.* Copyright © 1949 by Gwendolyn Brooks Blakely. Reprinted by permission of Harper & Row, Publishers, Inc.

To Houghton Mifflin Company for:

"To a Friend Whose Work Has Come to Triumph" from *All My Pretty Ones.* Copyright © 1961, 1962 by Anne Sexton. Reprinted by permission of the publisher, Houghton Mifflin Company.

"You, Doctor Martin" and "Her Kind" from *To Bedlam and Part Way Back*, copyright © 1960 by Anne Sexton. Reprinted by permission of the publisher, Houghton Mifflin Company.

"Vapor Trail Reflected in the Frog Pond" and "The Bear" from *Body Rags.* Copyright © 1965, 1966, 1967 by Galway Kinnell. Reprinted by permission of the publisher, Houghton Mifflin Company.

"You, Andrew Marvell," "The End of the World," and "Not Marble nor the Gilded Monuments" from *Collected Poems 1917–1952,* copyright © 1955 by Archibald MacLeish. Reprinted by permission of the publisher, Houghton Mifflin Company.

To Simon and Schuster for:

"Drinking Song" and "Awake" from *Outlyer and Ghazals* by Jim Harrison. Copyright © 1969, 1971 by Jim Harrison. Reprinted by permission of Simon and Schuster.

To Wesleyan University Press for:

"The Gallery," copyright © 1958 by Barbara Howes. Reprinted from *Light and Dark* by Barbara Howes, by permission of Wesleyan University Press. This poem was first published in *The New Yorker.*

"The Firebombing." Copyright © 1964 by James Dickey. Reprinted from *Buckdancer's Choice*, by James Dickey, by permission of Wesleyan University Press. This poem first appeared in *Poetry.*

"Beginning," "Mary Bly" and "A Blessing." Copyright © 1961, 1963 by James Wright. Reprinted from *This Branch Will Not Break*, by James Wright, by permission of Wesleyan University Press. "A Blessing" was first published in *Poetry.*

"Talking to Animals." Copyright © 1970 by Barbara Howes. Reprinted from *Blue Garden* by Barbara Howes, by permission of Wesleyan University Press.

The following poems by May Swenson are reprinted by permission of Charles Scribner's Sons.

"The Lightning" which appeared first in *Hudson Review* (copyright © 1965 May Swenson) from *Half Sun Half Sleep.*

"Trinity Churchyard, Spring 1961" (copyright © 1960 May Swenson) from *To Mix With Time.*

"Sun" (copyright © 1949 May Swenson) from *To Mix With Time.*

To Doubleday and Company for:

"Cuttings," by Theodore Roethke. Copyright 1948 by Theodore Roethke, "Elegy for Jane." Copyright 1950 by Theodore Roethke; "In a Dark Time" by Theodore Roethke. Copyright © 1960 by Beatrice Roethke, Administratrix of the estate of Theodore Roethke. From *Collected Poems of Theodore Roethke* by Theodore Roethke. Reprinted by permission of Doubleday and Company, Inc.

To University of North Carolina Press for:

"A Sentimental Delusion" and "An Annual & Perennial Problem" from *A Time of Bees* by Mona Van Duyn. Published by University of North Carolina Press, 1964. Reprinted by permission of the publisher.

A FOREWORD

In the half-century between 1920 and 1970 the writing of poetry in the English language underwent radical changes in style and sensibility. Such established poets as Frost, Stevens, Pound, and Eliot were producing some of their most characteristic work, but another generation was composing poetry with another consciousness, a new tone as well as a new technique. In those fifty years the fifty poets included in this volume attained an unprecedented range and diversity. The gamut was all the way from immediately communicated verse in traditional forms to indirect and difficult innovations in fluid movement and free association. The very mutability of styles was one of the features of the era.

Much of the poetry seemed improvisational, the dictates of a "stream of consciousness" boldly adventurous in subject matter and treatment. Much of it, complying with the demand for new words to express a new age, was marked by startling unions, sudden leaps from one image to another, and by uncommon juxtapositions that dispensed with logical connections. Some of the most colorful effects were achieved by nonsequiturs and the esthetic shocks of surrealism (often dismissed as irrationalism) and by multiple levels of meaning, confirming the claim that the creative process functioned freely in ambiguities.

If the attitude frequently assumed was an existentialist acceptance of a universe indifferent to the individual, it was counterbalanced by a feeling, often a passionate concern, for what had hitherto been regarded as material too unpoetic for poetry. Most of the modern poets accepted all aspects of reality, sordid as well as striking, and luxuriated in the complexity of the modern world. Old forms were refreshed with new idioms; a loose rhetoric was followed by a return to precision. There were those who insisted that any discipline was an inhibition that fettered free expression, and there were those who believed with Thoreau that art, like life, is at its height when it is subject to the highest discipline.

It is a truism that all the arts are in a perpetual state of rotation: a swing to and from convention and revolt. Modern poetry is no exception. It continually alternates between traditional and experimental modes. The moot matter of formal versus nonformal verse was projected in a concise and cogent, as well as amusing, metaphor by Greg Kuzma in the December 1971 issue of *Poetry*. Logically entitled "Poetry," it maintained that

> The old forms are like birdhouses that
> have been made homes so long they are
> full of stuffing. Only the rarest birds
> can squeeze in and out of the doorways. And
> then they can't move around much inside, but
> keep peeping the same sounds. Which the
> stuffing almost insulates. But
> still they stay stuck, up on their poles.
> And we keep listening hard for voices
> to come out of them. And they do.

The place of the poet in today's world is an ambivalent one. On one hand he feels himself dedicated to convey what is beautiful or exalted or hopeful. On the other hand he is faced with a world torn by tensions, split by hatreds, threatened with annihilation. Yet he is, as Wordsworth said, a man speaking—or trying to speak—to men, directing them "to the things of everyday by awakening the mind's attention to the lethargy of custom," telling them that whatever its form or apparent formlessness, poetry is their common language, a language uplifted and intensified by emotion.

The poets represented in this book attempt to do, and often succeed in doing, what poetry has always attempted to do: to bring clarity out of confusion and, somehow, express the inexpressible in terms of the unforgettable. Probing, sometimes painfully, they reveal the varieties of the human condition with sensitivity and fresh perceptions.

Rather than interrupt the progress of the poems with prose commentaries—a progress in which a representation of the older poets serves as a bridge for the younger poets—the biographical and critical notes are in the back of the volume, chronologically arranged, beginning on page 225. The commentaries do not pretend to be the sole interpretation of the poets' intentions. They are meant to serve only as clues to understanding and guides to the associations of the poetry.

CONTENTS

II THE COMMENTARY

I THE POETRY

ROBERT FROST
1874-1963

MENDING WALL

Something there is that doesn't love a wall,
That sends the frozen-ground-swell under it,
And spills the upper boulders in the sun;
And makes gaps even two can pass abreast.
The work of hunters is another thing:
I have come after them and made repair
Where they have left not one stone on a stone,
But they would have the rabbit out of hiding,
To please the yelping dogs. The gaps I mean,
No one has seen them made or heard them made,
But at spring mending-time we find them there.
I let my neighbor know beyond the hill;
And on a day we meet to walk the line
And set the wall between us once again.
We keep the wall between us as we go.
To each the boulders that have fallen to each.
And some are loaves and some so nearly balls
We have to use a spell to make them balance:
"Stay where you are until our backs are turned!"
We wear our fingers rough with handling them.
Oh, just another kind of outdoor game,
One on a side. It comes to little more:
There where it is we do not need the wall:
He is all pine and I am apple orchard.
My apple trees will never get across
And eat the cones under his pines, I tell him.
He only says, "Good fences make good neighbors."
Spring is the mischief in me, and I wonder
If I could put a notion in his head:
"*Why* do they make good neighbors? Isn't it
Where there are cows? But here there are no cows.

Before I built a wall I'd ask to know
What I was walling in or walling out,
And to whom I was like to give offense.
Something there is that doesn't love a wall,
That wants it down." I could say "Elves" to him,
But it's not elves exactly, and I'd rather
He said it for himself. I see him there
Bringing a stone grasped firmly by the top
In each hand, like an old-stone savage armed.
He moves in darkness, as it seems to me,
Not of woods only and the shade of trees.
He will not go behind his father's saying,
And he likes having thought of it so well
He says again, "Good fences make good neighbors."

THE SILKEN TENT

She is as in a field a silken tent
At midday when a sunny summer breeze
Has dried the dew and all its ropes relent,
So that in guys it gently sways at ease,
And its supporting central cedar pole,
That is its pinnacle to heavenward
And signifies the sureness of the soul,
Seems to owe naught to any single cord,
But strictly held by none, is loosely bound
By countless silken ties of love and thought
To everything on earth the compass round,
And only by one's going slightly taut
In the capriciousness of summer air
Is of the slightest bondage made aware.

DIRECTIVE

Back out of all this now too much for us,
Back in a time made simple by the loss
Of detail, burned, dissolved, and broken off
Like graveyard marble sculpture in the weather,
There is a house that is no more a house
Upon a farm that is no more a farm
And in a town that is no more a town.
The road there, if you'll let a guide direct you
Who only has at heart your getting lost,
May seem as if it should have been a quarry—
Great monolithic knees the former town
Long since gave up pretence of keeping covered.
And there's a story in a book about it:
Besides the wear of iron wagon wheels
The ledges show lines ruled southeast northwest,
The chisel work of an enormous Glacier
That braced his feet against the Arctic Pole.
You must not mind a certain coolness from him
Still said to haunt this side of Panther Mountain.
Nor need you mind the serial ordeal
Of being watched from forty cellar holes
As if by eye pairs out of forty firkins.
As for the woods' excitement over you
That sends light rustle rushes to their leaves,
Charge that to upstart inexperience.
Where were they all not twenty years ago?
They think too much of having shaded out
A few old pecker-fretted apple trees.
Make yourself up a cheering song of how
Someone's road home from work this once was,
Who may be just ahead of you on foot
Or creaking with a buggy load of grain.

The height of the adventure is the height
Of country where two village cultures faded
Into each other. Both of them are lost.
And if you're lost enough to find yourself
By now, pull in your ladder road behind you
And put a sign up CLOSED to all but me.
Then make yourself at home. The only field
Now left's no bigger than a harness gall.
First there's the children's house of make believe,
Some shattered dishes underneath a pine,
The playthings in the playhouse of the children.
Weep for what little things could make them glad.
Then for the house that is no more a house,
But only a belilaced cellar hole,
Now slowly closing like a dent in dough.
This was no playhouse but a house in earnest.
Your destination and your destiny's
A brook that was the water of the house,
Cold as a spring as yet so near its source,
Too lofty and original to rage.
(We know the valley streams that when aroused
Will leave their tatters hung on barb and thorn.)
I have kept hidden in the instep arch
Of an old cedar at the waterside
A broken drinking goblet like the Grail
Under a spell so the wrong ones can't find it,
So can't get saved, as Saint Mark says they mustn't.
(I stole the goblet from the children's playhouse.)
Here are your waters and your watering place.
Drink and be whole again beyond confusion.

WALLACE STEVENS
1879-1955

PETER QUINCE AT THE CLAVIER

I

Just as my fingers on these keys
Make music, so the selfsame sounds
On my spirit make a music, too.

Music is feeling, then, not sound;
And thus it is that what I feel,
Here in this room, desiring you,

Thinking of your blue-shadowed silk,
Is music. It is like the strain
Waked in the elders by Susanna.

Of a green evening, clear and warm,
She bathed in her still garden, while
The red-eyed elders watching, felt

The basses of their beings throb
In witching chords, and their thin blood
Pulse pizzicati of Hosanna.

II

In the green water, clear and warm,
Susanna lay.
She searched
The touch of springs,
And found
Concealed imaginings.
She sighed,
For so much melody.

Upon the bank, she stood
In the cool
Of spent emotions.
She felt, among the leaves,
The dew
Of old devotions.

She walked upon the grass,
Still quavering.
The winds were like her maids,
On timid feet,
Fetching her woven scarves,
Yet wavering.

A breath upon her hand
Muted the night.
She turned—
A cymbal crashed,
And roaring horns.

III

Soon, with a noise like tambourines,
Came her attendant Byzantines.

They wondered why Susanna cried
Against the elders by her side;

And as they whispered, the refrain
Was like a willow swept by rain.

Anon, their lamps' uplifted flame
Revealed Susanna and her shame.

And then, the simpering Byzantines
Fled, with a noise like tambourines.

IV

Beauty is momentary in the mind—
The fitful tracing of a portal;
But in the flesh it is immortal.

The body dies; the body's beauty lives.
So evenings die, in their green going,
A wave, interminably flowing.
So gardens die, their meek breath scenting
The cowl of winter, done repenting.
So maidens die, to the auroral
Celebration of a maiden's choral.
Susanna's music touched the bawdy strings
Of those white elders; but, escaping,
Left only Death's ironic scraping.
Now, in its immortality, it plays
On the clear viol of her memory,
And makes a constant sacrament of praise.

THE POEMS OF OUR CLIMATE

I

Clear water in a brilliant bowl,
Pink and white carnations. The light
In the room more like a snowy air,
Reflecting snow. A newly-fallen snow
At the end of winter when afternoons return.
Pink and white carnations—one desires
So much more than that. The day itself
Is simplified: a bowl of white,
Cold, a cold porcelain, low and round,
With nothing more than the carnations there.

II

Say even that this complete simplicity
Stripped one of all one's torments, concealed
The evilly compounded, vital I
And made it fresh in a world of white,
A world of clear water, brilliant-edged,
Still one would want more, one would need more,
More than a world of white and snowy scents.

III

There would still remain the never-resting mind,
So that one would want to escape, come back
To what had been so long composed.
The imperfect is our paradise.
Note that, in this bitterness, delight,
Since the imperfect is so hot in us,
Lies in flawed words and stubborn sounds.

OF MODERN POETRY

The poem of the mind in the act of finding
What will suffice. It has not always had
To find: the scene was set; it repeated what
Was in the script.
Then the theatre was changed
To something else. Its past was a souvenir.
It has to be living, to learn the speech of the place.
It has to face the men of the time and to meet
The women of the time. It has to think about war
And it has to find what will suffice. It has
To construct a new stage. It has to be on that stage
And, like an insatiable actor, slowly and
With meditation, speak words that in the ear,
In the delicatest ear of the mind, repeat,
Exactly, that which it wants to hear, at the sound
Of which, an invisible audience listens,
Not to the play, but to itself, expressed
In an emotion as of two people, as of two
Emotions becoming one. The actor is
A metaphysician in the dark, twanging
An instrument, twanging a wiry string that gives
Sounds passing through sudden rightnesses, wholly
Containing the mind, below which it cannot descend,
Beyond which it has no will to rise.
It must
Be the finding of a satisfaction, and may
Be of a man skating, a woman dancing, a woman
Combing. The poem of the act of the mind.

WILLIAM CARLOS WILLIAMS 1883-1963

TRACT

I will teach you my townspeople
how to perform a funeral—
for you have it over a troop
of artists—
unless one should scour the world—
you have the ground sense necessary.

See! the hearse leads.
I begin with a design for a hearse.
For Christ's sake not black—
nor white either—and not polished!
Let it be weathered—like a farm wagon—
with gilt wheels (this could be
applied fresh at small expense)
or no wheels at all:
a rough dray to drag over the ground.

Knock the glass out!
My God—glass, my townspeople!
For what purpose? Is it for the dead
to look out or for us to see
how well he is housed or to see
the flowers or the lack of them—
or what?
To keep the rain and snow from him?
He will have a heavier rain soon:
pebbles and dirt and what not.
Let there be no glass—
and no upholstery, phew!
and no little brass rollers

and small easy wheels on the bottom—
my townspeople what are you thinking of?

A rough plain hearse then
with gilt wheels and no top at all.
On this the coffin lies
by its own weight.

No wreaths please—
especially no hot house flowers.
Some common memento is better,
something he prized and is known by:
his old clothes—a few books perhaps—
God knows what! You realize
how we are about these things
my townspeople—
something will be found—anything
even flowers if he had come to that.
So much for the hearse.

For heaven's sake though see to the driver!
Take off the silk hat! In fact
that's no place at all for him—
up there unceremoniously
dragging our friend out to his own dignity!
Bring him down—bring him down!
Low and inconspicuous! I'd not have him ride
on the wagon at all—damn him—
the undertaker's understrapper!
Let him hold the reins
and walk at the side
and inconspicuously too!

Then briefly as to yourselves:
Walk behind—as they do in France,

seventh class, or if you ride
Hell take curtains! Go with some show
of inconvenience; sit openly—
to the weather as to grief.
Or do you think you can shut grief in?
What—from us? We who have perhaps
nothing to lose? Share with us
share with us—it will be money
in your pockets.
                    Go now.
I think you are ready.

THE WIDOW'S LAMENT IN SPRINGTIME

Sorrow is my own yard
where the new grass
flames as it has flamed
often before but not
with the cold fire
that closes round me this year.
Thirtyfive years
I lived with my husband.
The plumtree is white today
with masses of flowers.
Masses of flowers
loaded the cherry branches
and color some bushes
yellow and some red
but the grief in my heart
is stronger than they
for though they were my joy
formerly, today I notice them
and turned away forgetting.
Today my son told me
that in the meadows,
at the edge of the heavy woods
in the distance, he saw
trees of white flowers.
I feel that I would like
to go there
and fall into those flowers
and sink into the marsh near them.

THE YACHTS

contend in a sea which the land partly encloses
shielding them from the too heavy blows
of an ungoverned ocean which when it chooses

tortures the biggest hulls, the best man knows
to pit against its beatings, and sinks them pitilessly.
Mothlike in mists, scintillant in the minute

brilliance of cloudless days, with broad bellying sails
they glide to the wind tossing green water
from their sharp prows while over them the crew crawls

ant like, solicitously grooming them, releasing,
making fast as they turn, lean far over and having
caught the wind again, side by side, head for the mark.

In a well guarded arena of open water surrounded by
lesser and greater craft which, sycophant, lumbering
and flittering follow them, they appear youthful, rare

as the light of a happy eye, live with the grace
of all that in the mind is feckless, free and
naturally to be desired. Now the sea which holds them

is moody, lapping their glossy sides, as if feeling
for some slightest flaw but fails completely.
Today no race. Then the wind comes again. The yachts

move, jockeying for a start, the signal is set and they
are off. Now the waves strike at them but they are too
well made, they slip through, though they take in canvas.

Arms with hands grasping seek to clutch at the prows.
Bodies thrown recklessly in the way are cut aside.
It is a sea of faces about them in agony, in despair

until the horror of the race dawns staggering the mind,
the whole sea become an entanglement of watery bodies
lost to the world bearing what they cannot hold. Broken,

beaten, desolate, reaching from the dead to be taken up
they cry out, failing, failing! their cries rising
in waves still as the skillful yachts pass over.

THESE

are the desolate, dark weeks
when nature in its barrenness
equals the stupidity of man.

The year plunges into night
and the heart plunges
lower than night

to an empty, windswept place
without sun, stars or moon
but a peculiar light as of thought

that spins a dark fire—
whirling upon itself until,
in the cold, it kindles

to make a man aware of nothing
that he knows, not loneliness
itself—Not a ghost but

would be embraced—emptiness,
despair—(They
whine and whistle) among

the flashes and booms of war;
houses of whose rooms
the cold is greater than can be thought,

the people gone that we loved,
the beds lying empty, the couches
damp, the chairs unused—

Hide it away somewhere
out of the mind, let it get roots
and grow, unrelated to jealous

ears and eyes—for itself.
In this mine they come to dig—all.
Is this the counterfoil to sweetest

music? The source of poetry that
seeing the clock stopped, says,
The clock has stopped

that ticked yesterday so well?
and hears the sound of lakewater
splashing—that is now stone.

ANNA WICKHAM
1884-1947

THE FIRED POT

In our town, people live in rows.
The only irregular thing in a street is the steeple;
And where that points to God only knows,
And not the poor disciplined people!

And I have watched the women growing old,
Passionate about pins, and pence, and soap,
Till the heart within my wedded breast grew cold,
And I lost hope.

But a young soldier came to our town,
He spoke his mind most candidly.
He asked me quickly to lie down,
And that was very good for me.

For though I gave him no embrace—
Remembering my duty—
He altered the expression of my face,
And gave me back my beauty.

SELF-ANALYSIS

The tumult of my fretted mind
Gives me expression of a kind;
But it is faulty, harsh, not plain—
My work has the incompetence of pain.

I am consumed with slow fire,
For righteousness is my desire;
Towards that good goal I cannot whip my will,
I am a tired horse that jibs upon a hill.

I desire Virtue, though I love her not—
I have no faith in her when she is got:
I fear that she will bind and make me slave,
And send me songless to the sullen grave.

I am like a man who fears to take a wife,
And frets his soul with wantons all his life.
With rich, unholy foods I stuff my maw;
When I am sick, then I believe in law.

I fear the whiteness of straight ways—
I think there is no colour in unsullied days.
My silly sins I take for my heart's ease,
And know my beauty—in the end—disease.

Of old there were great heroes, strong in fight,
Who, tense and sinless, kept a fire alight:
God of our hope, in their great name,
Give me the straight and ordered flame.

MEDITATION AT KEW

Alas! for all the pretty women who marry dull men,
Go into the suburbs and never come out again,
Who lose their pretty faces and dim their pretty eyes,
Because no one has skill or courage to organize.

What do these pretty women suffer when they marry?
They bear a boy who is like Uncle Harry,
A girl who is like Aunt Eliza, and not new,
These old dull races must breed true.

I would enclose a common in the sun,
And let the young wives out to laugh and run;
I would steal their dull clothes and go away,
And leave the pretty naked things to play.

Then I would make a contract with hard Fate
That they see all the men in the world and choose a mate,
And I would summon all the pipers in the town
That they dance with Love at a feast, and dance him down.

From the gay unions of choice
We'd have a race of splendid beauty and of thrilling voice.
The World whips frank, gay love with rods,
But frankly gaily shall we get the gods.

A LOVE LETTER

You have given me some quality of the male,
While I have given you some qualities of myself.
You are the father of my action,
While I have begotten in you new courage.
Maybe we are completed by love,
So that we are beyond sex.
We have found the miraculous unity,
To which existence itself implies increase.

I do not grieve away my days
Because you are gone from me,
My mind is stimulated forever by the idea of you,
I do not ask that your love should be faithful to my body,
It is impossible that your soul should be faithless to my soul.

It is well I cannot eat with you all my days,
I would not take my soup from a consecrated cup.
I have before me a wealth of happy moments when I shall see
you.
They are like holy wafers, which I will eat,
For stimulation, for absolution, and for my eternal hope.

I ask nothing of you, not even that you live.
If you die, I remember you
Till the blood in my wrists is cold.

EZRA POUND
1885-1972

PORTRAIT D'UNE FEMME

Your mind and you are our Sargasso Sea,
London has swept about you this score years
And bright ships left you this or that in fee:
Ideas, old gossip, oddments of all things,
Strange spars of knowledge and dimmed wares of price.
Great minds have sought you—lacking someone else.
You have been second always. Tragical?
No. You preferred it to the usual thing:
One dull man, dulling and uxorious,
One average mind—with one thought less, each year.
Oh, you are patient, I have seen you sit
Hours, where something might have floated up.
And now you pay one. Yes, you richly pay.
You are a person of some interest, one comes to you
And takes strange gain away:
Trophies fished up; some curious suggestion;
Fact that leads nowhere; and a tale or two,
Pregnant with mandrakes, or with something else
That might prove useful and yet never proves,
That never fits a corner or shows use,
Or finds its hour upon the loom of days:
The tarnished, gaudy, wonderful old work;
Idols and ambergris and rare inlays,
These are your riches, your great store; and yet
For all this sea-hoard of deciduous things,
Strange woods half sodden, and new brighter stuff:
In the slow float of different light and deep,
No! there is nothing! In the whole and all,
Nothing that's quite your own.
Yet this is you.

THE REST

O helpless few in my country,
O remnant enslaved!

Artists broken against her,
A-stray, lost in the villages,
Mistrusted, spoken-against,

Lovers of beauty, starved,
Thwarted with systems,
Helpless against the control;

You who can not wear yourselves out
By persisting to successes,
You who can only speak,
Who can not steel yourselves into reiteration;

You of the finer sense,
Broken against false knowledge,
You who can know at first hand,
Hated, shut in, mistrusted:

Take thought:
I have weathered the storm,
I have beaten out my exile.

THE LAKE ISLE

O God, O Venus, O Mercury, patron of thieves,
Give me in due time, I beseech you, a little tobacco-shop,
With the little bright boxes
          piled up neatly upon the shelves
And the loose fragrant cavendish
          and the shag,
And the bright Virginia
          loose under the bright glass cases,
And a pair of scales not too greasy,
And the whores dropping in for a word or two in passing,
For a flip word, and to tidy their hair a bit.

O God, O Venus, O Mercury, patron of thieves,
Lend me a little tobacco-shop,
          or install me in any profession
Save this damn'd profession of writing,
          where one needs one's brains all the time.

MARIANNE MOORE
1887-1972

NEVERTHELESS

you've seen a strawberry
that's had a struggle; yet
was, where the fragments met,

a hedgehog or a star-
fish for the multitude
of seeds. What better food

than apple-seeds—the fruit
within the fruit—locked in
like counter-curved twin

hazel-nuts? Frost that kills
the little rubber-plant-
leaves of *kok-saghyz*-stalks, can't

harm the roots; they still grow
in frozen ground. Once where
there was a prickly-pear-

leaf clinging to barbed wire,
a root shot down to grow
in earth two feet below;

as carrots form mandrakes
or a ram's-horn root sometimes. Victory won't come

to me unless I go
to it; a grape-tendril
ties a knot in knots till

knotted thirty times,—so
    the bound twig that's under-
    gone and over-gone, can't stir.

The weak overcomes its
    menace, the strong over-
    comes itself. What is there

like fortitude! What sap
    went through that little thread
    to make the cherry red!

THE MIND IS AN ENCHANTING THING

is an enchanted thing
    like the glaze on a
katydid-wing
        subdivided by sun
        till the nettings are legion.
Like Gieseking playing Scarlatti;

like the apteryx-awl
    as a beak, or the
kiwi's rain-shawl
        of haired feathers, the mind
        feeling its way as though blind,
walks along with its eyes on the ground.

It has memory's ear
    that can hear without
having to hear.
        Like the gyroscope's fall,
        truly unequivocal
because trued by regnant certainty,

it is a power of
    strong enchantment. It
is like the dove-
        neck animated by
        sun; it is memory's eye;
it's conscientious inconsistency.

It tears off the veil; tears
    the temptation, the
mist the heart wears,

from its eyes,—if the heart
has a face; it takes apart
dejection. It's fire in the dove-neck's

iridescence; in the
inconsistencies
of Scarlatti.
Unconfusion submits
its confusion to proof; it's
not a Herod's oath that cannot change.

THE WOOD-WEASEL

emerges daintily, the skunk—
don't laugh—in sylvan black and white chipmunk
regalia. The inky thing
adaptively whited with glistening
goat-fur, is wood-warden. In his
ermined well-cuttlefish-inked wool, he is
determination's totem. Out-
lawed? His sweet face and powerful feet go about
in chieftain's coat of Chilcat cloth.
He is his own protection from the moth,

noble little warrior. That
otter-skin on it, the living pole-cat,
smothers anything that stings. Well,—
this same weasel's playful and his weasel
associates are too. Only
wood-weasels shall associate with me.

THE HOLLOW MEN

Mistah Kurtz—he dead.
A penny for the Old Guy.

I

We are the hollow men
We are the stuffed men
Leaning together
Headpiece filled with straw. Alas!
Our dried voices, when
We whisper together
Are quiet and meaningless
As wind in dry grass
Or rats' feet over broken glass
In our dry cellar

Shape without form, shade without colour,
Paralysed force, gesture without motion;

Those who have crossed
With direct eyes, to death's other Kingdom
Remember us—if at all—not as lost
Violent souls, but only
As the hollow men
The stuffed men.

II

Eyes I dare not meet in dreams
In death's dream kingdom
These do not appear:
There, the eyes are
Sunlight on a broken column

There, is a tree swinging
And voices are
In the wind's singing
More distant and more solemn
Than a fading star.

Let me be no nearer
In death's dream kingdom
Let me also wear
Such deliberate disguises
Rat's skin, crowskin, crossed staves
In a field
Behaving as the wind behaves
No nearer—

Not that final meeting
In the twilight kingdom

III

This is the dead land
This is cactus land
Here the stone images
Are raised, here they receive
The supplication of a dead man's hand
Under the twinkle of a fading star.

Is it like this
In death's other kingdom
Waking alone
At the hour when we are
Trembling with tenderness
Lips that would kiss
Form prayers to broken stone.

IV

The eyes are not here
There are no eyes here
In this valley of dying stars
In this hollow valley
This broken jaw of our lost kingdoms

In this last of meeting places
We grope together
And avoid speech
Gathered on this beach of the tumid river

Sightless, unless
The eyes reappear
As the perpetual star
Multifoliate rose
Of death's twilight kingdom
The hope only
Of empty men.

V

Here we go round the prickly pear
Prickly pear prickly pear
Here we go round the prickly pear
At five o'clock in the morning.

Between the idea
And the reality
Between the motion
And the act
Falls the Shadow

For Thine is the Kingdom

Between the conception
And the creation
Between the emotion
And the response
Falls the Shadow
Life is very long

Between the desire
And the spasm
Between the potency
And the existence
Between the essence
And the descent
Falls the Shadow
For Thine is the Kingdom

For Thine is
Life is
For Thine is the

This is the way the world ends
This is the way the world ends
This is the way the world ends
Not with a bang but a whimper.

CHORUS FROM "THE ROCK"

The Word of the LORD came unto me, saying:
O miserable cities of designing men,
O wretched generation of enlightened men,
Betrayed in the mazes of your ingenuities,
Sold by the proceeds of your proper inventions:
I have given you hands which you turn from worship,
I have given you speech, for endless palaver,
I have given you my Law, and you set up commissions,
I have given you lips, to express friendly sentiments,
I have given you hearts, for reciprocal distrust.
I have given you power of choice, and you only alternate
Between futile speculation and unconsidered action.
Many are engaged in writing books and printing them,
Many desire to see their names in print,
Many read nothing but the race reports.
Much is your reading, but not the Word of GOD,
Much is your building, but not the House of GOD.
Will you build me a house of plaster, with corrugated roofing,
To be filled with a litter of Sunday newspapers?

1ST MALE VOICE:
A Cry from the East:
What shall be done to the shore of smoky ships?
Will you leave my people forgetful and forgotten
To idleness, labour, and delirious stupor?
There shall be left the broken chimney,
The peeled hull, a pile of rusty iron,
In a street of scattered brick where the goat climbs,
Where My Word is unspoken.

2ND MALE VOICE:

A Cry from the North, from the West and from the South
Whence thousands travel daily to the timekept City;
Where My Word is unspoken,
In the land of lobelias and tennis flannels
The rabbit shall burrow and the thorn revisit,
The nettle shall flourish on the gravel court,
And the wind shall say: "Here were decent god-less people:
Their only monument the asphalt road
And a thousand lost golf balls."

JOURNEY OF THE MAGI

"A COLD coming we had of it,
Just the worst time of the year
For a journey, and such a long journey:
The ways deep and the weather sharp,
The very dead of winter."
And the camels galled, sore-footed, refractory,
Lying down in the melting snow.
There were times we regretted
The summer palaces on slopes, the terraces,
And the silken girls bringing sherbet.
Then the camel men cursing and grumbling
And running away, and wanting their liquor and women,
And the night-fires going out, and the lack of shelters,
And the cities hostile and the towns unfriendly
And the villages dirty and charging high prices:
A hard time we had of it.
At the end we preferred to travel all night,
Sleeping in snatches,
With the voices singing in our ears, saying
That this was all folly.

Then at dawn we came down to a temperate valley,
Wet, below the snow line, smelling of vegetation;
With a running stream and a water-mill beating the darkness,
And three trees on the low sky,
And an old white horse galloped away in the meadow.
Then we came to a tavern with vine-leaves over the lintel,
Six hands at an open door dicing for pieces of silver,
And feet kicking the empty wine-skins.
But there was no information, and so we continued
And arrived at evening, not a moment too soon
Finding the place; it was (you may say) satisfactory.

All this was a long time ago, I remember,
And I would do it again, but set down
This set down
This: were we led all that way for
Birth or Death? There was a Birth, certainly,
We had evidence and no doubt. I had seen birth and death,
But had thought they were different; this Birth was
Hard and bitter agony for us, like Death, our death.
We returned to our places, these Kingdoms,
But no longer at ease here, in the old dispensation,
With an alien people clutching their gods.
I should be glad of another death.

CONRAD AIKEN
1889-

A LETTER FROM THE GRASS

Indeed, child, the little pimpernel, most modest
and obscure of flowers, which here you see
between the tree-roots, the tiny star
of dusty red, or is it vermilion, each petal
with a most delicate point, and the clouded center,
and, yes, like something one might discover
coming through the far eye of a telescope
on a blue night in summer—indeed this little flower
will speak to us if we will listen.
It will say

something of the noiseless unfolding of the shutters of daybreak
in the great silence of morning, something too
of the manifold infoldings of nightfall: it will praise
with its own voice, its own small voice, but no less clear
or dear for that, the infinitesimal
tickling and tinklings of its beginnings,
when the pale root-foot breaks the seed
to adventure downward into darkness, while the pale stalk,
longing to be green, to be green, yearns itself upward
to salute with its new hands the sun.
It will say

that life is whole, although it be but for a day
of one's own circling with the circling world
until the shut-eye planets bid us to sleep.
One day, and we have learned it all,
from the first feathered shadow's fall,
whether from tree or garden wall,
until once more the invisible ladder
of sunlight climbs to noon. And so revolving,

and so returning with our praise, until that time
when again shadows with the dead moon climb.
Now its eye opens, then it will close.
And this is what it knows.

THE CENSUS-TAKERS

Stranger, did you ever play ball in a vacant lot?
Will you lend us the loan of a match? or spare us a dime?
Did you hear of the murder? Would you like us to show you the spot?
Or like us to re-enact—on the spot—the crime?

Did you play ground-cricket by the light of the stars with a stick—
Tapped from the curb and tipped out of sight in the sky?
Was the street ever covered with straw when your mother was sick?
Will you visit the Funeral Home, and alone, when you die?

Over which shoulder, stranger, do you squint at the moon?
And where is the ferry, that meets you at half-past six?
What time is it now by the heart—too late? Too soon?
Will you hurry and tell us? That river, down there, is the Styx—

And we are the census-takers; the questions that ask
from corner and street, from lamp-post and sign and face;
The questions that later tonight will take you to task,
When you sit down alone, to think, in a lonely place.

Did you ever play blind-man's buff in the bat-flit light?
Stranger, whose heart did you break? and what else did you do?—
The census-takers are coming to ask you tonight;
The truth will be hurrying home, and it's time you knew.

ARCHIBALD MACLEISH
1892-

YOU, ANDREW MARVELL

And here face down beneath the sun
And here upon earth's noonward height
To feel the always coming on
The always rising of the night:

To feel creep up the curving east
The earthy chill of dusk and slow
Upon those under lands the vast
And ever climbing shadow grow

And strange at Ecbatan the trees
Take leaf by leaf the evening strange
The flooding dark about their knees
The mountains over Persia change

And now at Kermanshah the gate
Dark empty and the withered grass
And through the twilight now the late
Few travelers in the westward pass

And Baghdad darken and the bridge
Across the silent river gone
And through Arabia the edge
Of evening widen and steal on

And deepen on Palmyra's street
The wheel rut in the ruined stone
And Lebanon fade out and Crete
High through the clouds and overblown

And over Sicily the air
Still flashing with the landward gulls
And loom and slowly disappear
The sails above the shadowy hulls

And Spain go under and the shore
Of Africa the gilded sand
And evening vanish and no more
The low pale light across that land

Nor now the long light on the sea:

And here face downward in the sun
To feel how swift how secretly
The shadow of the night comes on . . .

THE END OF THE WORLD

Quite unexpectedly as Vasserot
The armless ambidextrian was lighting
A match between his great and second toe
And Ralph the lion was engaged in biting
The neck of Madame Sossman while the drum
Pointed, and Teeny was about to cough
In waltz-time swinging Jocko by the thumb—
Quite unexpectedly the top blew off:

And there, there overhead, there, there, hung over
Those thousands of white faces, those dazed eyes,
There in the starless dark the poise, the hover,
There with vast wings across the canceled skies,
There in the sudden blackness the black pall
Of nothing, nothing, nothing—nothing at all.

"NOT MARBLE NOR THE GILDED MONUMENTS"

for Adele

The praisers of women in their proud and beautiful poems,
Naming the grave mouth and the hair and the eyes,
Boasted those they loved should be forever remembered:
These were lies.

The words sound but the face in the Istrian sun is forgotten.
The poet speaks but to her dead ears no more.
The sleek throat is gone—and the breast that was troubled to
listen:
Shadow from door.

Therefore I will not praise your knees nor your fine walking
Telling you men shall remember your name as long
As lips move or breath is spent or the iron of English
Rings from a tongue.

I shall say you were young, and your arms straight, and your
mouth scarlet:
I shall say you will die and none will remember you:
Your arms change, and none remember the swish of your gar-
ments,
Nor the click of your shoe.

Not with my hand's strength, not with difficult labor
Springing the obstinate words to the bones of your breast
And the stubborn line to your young stride and the breath to your
breathing
And the beat to your haste
Shall I prevail on the hearts of unborn men to remember.

(What is a dead girl but a shadowy ghost
Or a dead man's voice but a distant and vain affirmation
Like dream words most)

Therefore I will not speak of the undying glory of women.
I will say you were young and straight and your skin fair
And you stood in the door and the sun was a shadow of leaves on
    your shoulders
And a leaf on your hair—

I will not speak of the famous beauty of dead women:
I will say the shape of a leaf lay once on your hair.
Till the world ends and the eyes are out and the mouths broken
Look! It is there!

E. E. CUMMINGS
1894-1962

my father moved through dooms of love

my father moved through dooms of love
through sames of am through haves of give,
singing each morning out of each night
my father moved through depths of height

this motionless forgetful where
turned at his glance to shining here;
that if (so timid air is firm)
under his eyes would stir and squirm

newly as from unburied which
floats the first who, his april touch
drove sleeping selves to swarm their fates
woke dreamers to their ghostly roots

and should some why completely weep
my father's fingers brought her sleep:
vainly no smallest voice might cry
for he could feel the mountains grow.

Lifting the valleys of the sea
my father moved through griefs of joy;
praising a forehead called the moon
singing desire into begin

joy was his song and joy so pure
a heart of star by him could steer
and pure so now and now so yes
the wrists of twilight would rejoice

keen as midsummer's keen beyond
conceiving mind of sun will stand,
so strictly (over utmost him
so hugely) stood my father's dream

his flesh was flesh his blood was blood:
no hungry man but wished him food;
no cripple wouldn't creep one mile
uphill to only see him smile.

Scorning the pomp of must and shall
my father moved through dooms of feel;
his anger was as right as rain
his pity was as green as grain

septembering arms of year extend
less humbly wealth to foe and friend
than he to foolish and to wise
offered immeasurable is

proudly and (by octobering flame
beckoned) as earth will downward climb,
so naked for immortal work
his shoulders marched against the dark

his sorrow was as true as bread:
no liar looked him in the head;
if every friend became his foe
he'd laugh and build a world with snow.

My father moved through theys of we,
singing each new leaf out of each tree
(and every child was sure that spring
danced when she heard my father sing)

then let men kill which cannot share,
let blood and flesh be mud and mire,
scheming imagine,passion willed,
freedom a drug that's bought and sold

giving to steal and cruel kind,
a heart to fear,to doubt a mind,
to differ a disease of same,
conform the pinnacle of am

though dull were all we taste as bright,
bitter all utterly things sweet,
maggoty minus and dumb death
all we inherit,all bequeath

and nothing quite so least as truth
—i say though hate were why men breathe—
because my father lived his soul
love is the whole and more than all

now that, more nearest even than your fate

now that,more nearest even than your fate

and mine(or any truth beyond perceive)
quivers this miracle of summer night

her trillion secrets touchably alive

—while and all mysteries which i or you
(blinded by merely things believable)
could only fancy we should never know

are unimaginably ours to feel—

how should some world(we marvel)doubt,for just
sweet terrifying the particular
moment it takes one very falling most
(there:did you see it?)star to disappear,

that hugest whole creation may be less
incalculable than a single kiss

HART CRANE
1899-1932

VOYAGES: II

And yet this great wink of eternity,
Of rimless floods, unfettered leewardings,
Samite sheeted and processioned where
Her undinal vast belly moonward bends,
Laughing the wrapt inflections of our love;

Take this Sea, whose diapason knells
On scrolls of silver snowy sentences,
The sceptred terror of whose sessions rends
As her demeanors motion well or ill,
All but the pieties of lovers' hands.

And onward, as bells off San Salvador
Salute the crocus lustres of the stars,
In these poinsettia meadows of her tides,—
Adagios of islands, O my Prodigal,
Complete the dark confessions her veins spell.

Mark how her turning shoulders wind the hours,
And hasten while her penniless rich palms
Pass superscription of bent foam and wave,—
Hasten, while they are true,—sleep, death, desire,
Close round one instant in one floating flower.

Bind us in time, O Seasons clear, and awe.
O minstrel galleons of Carib fire,
Bequeath us to no earthly shore until
Is answered in the vortex of our grave
The seal's wide spindrift gaze toward paradise.

THE BROKEN TOWER

The bell-rope that gathers God at dawn
Dispatches me as though I dropped down the knell
Of a spent day—to wander the cathedral lawn
From pit to crucifix, feet chill on steps from hell.

Have you not heard, have you not seen that corps
Of shadows in the tower, whose shoulders sway
Antiphonal carillons launched before
The stars are caught and hived in the sun's ray?

The bells, I say, the bells break down their tower;
And swing I know not where. Their tongues engrave
Membrane through marrow, my long-scattered score
Of broken intervals. . . . And I, their sexton slave!

Oval encyclicals in canyons heaping
The impasse high with choir. Banked voices slain!
Pagodas, campaniles with reveilles outleaping—
O terraced echoes prostrate on the plain! . . .

And so it was I entered the broken world
To trace the visionary company of love, its voice
An instant in the wind (I know not whither hurled)
But not for long to hold each desperate choice.

My word I poured. But was it cognate, scored
Of that tribunal monarch of the air
Whose thigh embronzes earth, strikes crystal Word
In wounds pledged once to hope—cleft to despair?

The steep encroachments of my blood left me
No answer (could blood hold such a lofty tower

As flings the question true?)—or is it she
Whose sweet mortality stirs latent power?—

And through whose pulse I hear, counting the strokes
My veins recall and add, revived and sure
The angelus of wars my chest evokes:
What I hold healed, original now, and pure . . .

And builds, within, a tower that is not stone
(Not stone can jacket heaven)—but slip
Of pebbles—visible wings of silence sown
In azure circles, widening as they dip

The matrix of the heart, lift down the eye
That shrines the quiet lake and swells a tower . . .
The commodious, tall decorum of that sky
Unseals her earth, and lifts love in its shower.

LANGSTON HUGHES
1902-1967

YOUNG GAL'S BLUES

I'm gonna walk to the graveyard
'Hind ma friend Miss Cora Lee.
Gonna walk to the graveyard
'Hind ma dear friend Cora Lee
Cause when I'm dead some
Body'll have to walk behind me.

I'm goin' to the po' house
To see ma old Aunt Clew.
Goin' to the po' house
To see ma old Aunt Clew.
When I'm old an' ugly
I'll want to see somebody, too.

The po' house is lonely
An' the grave is cold.
O, the po' house is lonely,
The graveyard grave is cold.
But I'd rather be dead than
To be ugly an' old.

When love is gone what
Can a young gal do?
When love is gone, O,
What can a young gal do?
Keep on a-lovin' me, daddy,
Cause I don't want to be blue.

MADAM AND THE RENT MAN

The rent man knocked.
He said, Howdy-do?
I said, What
Can I do for you?
He said, You know
Your rent is due.

I said, Listen,
Before I'd pay
I'd go to Hades
And rot away.

The sink is broke,
The water don't run,
And you ain't done a thing
You promised to've done.

Back window's cracked,
Kitchen floor squeaks,
There's rats in the cellar,
And the attic leaks.

He said, Madam,
It's not up to me.
I'm just the agent,
Don't you see?

I said, Naturally,
You pass the buck.
If it's money you want,
You're out of luck.

He said, Madam, I ain't pleased.
I said, Neither am I.

So we agrees.

RICHARD EBERHART
1904-

THE GROUNDHOG

In June, amid the golden fields,
I saw a groundhog lying dead.
Dead lay he; my senses shook,
And mind outshot our naked frailty.
There lowly in the vigorous summer
His form began its senseless change,
And made my senses waver dim
Seeing nature ferocious in him.
Inspecting close his maggots' might
And seething cauldron of his being,
Half with loathing, half with a strange love,
I poked him with an angry stick.
The fever arose, became a flame
And Vigour circumscribed the skies,
Immense energy in the sun,
And through my frame a sunless trembling.
My stick had done nor good nor harm.
Then stood I silent in the day
Watching the object, as before;
And kept my reverence for knowledge
Trying for control, to be still,
To quell the passion of the blood;
Until I had bent down on my knees
Praying for joy in the sight of decay.
And so I left; and I returned
In Autumn strict of eye, to see
The sap gone out of the groundhog,
But the bony sodden hulk remained.
But the year had lost its meaning,
And in intellectual chains
I lost both love and loathing,

Mured up in the wall of wisdom.
Another summer took the fields again
Massive and burning, full of life,
But when I chanced upon the spot
There was only a little hair left,
And bones bleaching in the sunlight
Beautiful as architecture;
I watched them like a geometer,
And cut a walking stick from a birch.

It has been three years now.
There is no sign of the groundhog.
I stood there in the whirling summer,
My hand capped a withered heart,
And thought of China and of Greece,
Of Alexander in his tent,
Of Montaigne in his tower,
Of Saint Theresa in her wild lament.

IF I COULD ONLY LIVE AT THE PITCH THAT IS NEAR MADNESS

If I could only live at the pitch that is near madness
When everything is as it was in my childhood
Violent, vivid, and of infinite possibility:
That the sun and the moon broke over my head.

Then I cast time out of the trees and fields,
Then I stood immaculate in the Ego;
Then I eyed the world with all delight,
Reality was the perfection of my sight.

And time has big handles on the hands,
Fields and trees a way of being themselves.
I saw battalions of the race of mankind
Standing stolid, demanding a moral answer.

I gave the moral answer and I died
And into a realm of complexity came
Where nothing is possible but necessity
And the truth wailing there like a red babe.

MAN AND NATURE

Man is the writing instrument
who thinks that he impresses nature.
He perceives the sense of the sea
As if for the first time.
It was so decades ago.
He sits as a contemplator
In secret frenzies of realization,
The islands are the same,
In the spirit of indifference.

He leans forward in his seat.
He has faced the headlands.
It is a place too pure to be true.
The tensions of his spirit leap
Looking into ultimate ocean
Beyond Spectacle, Pond, and Hog.
There on the horizon Eagle Island
Light and the open Atlantic
Deceive him again with thought.

The summer trees, the birds, the bees
Eradicate fate of timelessness
In high July, but not for long.
The long thoughts are beyond.
As he looks outward to the oceanic,
Beyond a child coming in the door,
Beyond the self, beyond desire,
He breathes the universe,
In, continuance, out, salutations.

STANLEY KUNITZ
1905-

THE WAR AGAINST THE TREES

The man who sold his lawn to standard oil
Joked with his neighbors come to watch the show
While the bulldozers, drunk with gasoline,
Tested the virtue of the soil
Under the branchy sky
By overthrowing first the privet-row.

Forsythia-forays and hydrangea-raids
Were but preliminaries to a war
Against the great-grandfathers of the town,
So freshly lopped and maimed.
They struck and struck again,
And with each elm a century went down.

All day the hireling engines charged the trees,
Subverting them by hacking underground
In grub-dominions, where dark summer's mole
Rampages through his halls,
Till a northern seizure shook
Those crowns, forcing the giants to their knees.

I saw the ghosts of children at their games
Racing beyond their childhood in the shade,
And while the green world turned its death-foxed page
And a red wagon wheeled,
I watched them disappear
Into the suburbs of their grievous age.

Ripped from the craters much too big for hearts
The club-roots bared their amputated coils,
Raw gorgons matted blind, whose pocks and scars

Cried Moon! on a corner lot
One witness-moment, caught
In the rear-view mirrors of the passing cars.

THE PORTRAIT

My mother never forgave my father
for killing himself,
especially at such an awkward time
and in a public park,
that spring
when I was waiting to be born.
She locked his name
in her deepest cabinet
and would not let him out,
though I could hear him thumping.
When I came down from the attic
with the pastel portrait in my hand
of a long-lipped stranger
with a brave moustache
and deep brown level eyes,
she ripped it into shreds
without a single word
and slapped me hard.
In my sixty-fourth year
I can feel my cheek
still burning.

A. D. HOPE
1907-

IMPERIAL ADAM

Imperial Adam, naked in the dew,
Felt his brown flanks and found the rib was gone.
Puzzled he turned and saw where, two and two,
The mighty spoor of Jahweh marked the lawn.

Then he remembered through mysterious sleep
The surgeon fingers probing at the bone,
The voice so far away, so rich and deep:
"It is not good for him to live alone."

Turning once more he found Man's counterpart
In tender parody breathing at his side.
He knew her at first sight, he knew by heart
Her allegory of sense unsatisfied.

The pawpaw drooped its golden breasts above
Less generous than the honey of her flesh;
The innocent sunlight showed the place of love;
The dew on its dark hairs winked crisp and fresh.

This plump gourd severed from his virile root,
She promised on the turf of Paradise
Delicious pulp of the forbidden fruit;
Sly as the snake she loosed her sinuous thighs,

And waking, smiled up at him from the grass;
Her breasts rose softly and he heard her sigh—
From all the beasts whose pleasant task it was
In Eden to increase and multiply

Adam had learned the jolly deed of kind:
He took her in his arms and there and then,
Like the clean beasts, embracing from behind,
Began in joy to found the breed of men.

Then from the spurt of seed within her broke
Her terrible and triumphant female cry,
Split upward by the sexual lightning stroke.
It was the beasts now who stood watching by:

The gravid elephant, the calving hind,
The breeding bitch, the she-ape big with young
Were the first gentle midwives of mankind;
The teeming lioness rasped her with her tongue;

The proud vicuña nuzzled her as she slept
Lax on the grass; and Adam watching too
Saw how her dumb breasts at their ripening wept,
The great pod of her belly swelled and grew,

And saw its water break, and saw, in fear,
Its quaking muscles in the act of birth,
Between her legs a pigmy face appear,
And the first murderer lay upon the earth.

THE BRIDES

Down the assembly line they roll and pass
Complete at last, a miracle of design;
Their chromium fenders, the unbreakable glass,
The fashionable curve, the air-flow line.

Grease to the elbows Mum and Dad enthuse,
Pocket their spanners and survey the bride;
Murmur: "A sweet job! All she needs is juice!
Built for a life-time—sleek as a fish. Inside

"He will find every comfort: the full set
Of gadgets; knobs that answer to the touch
For light or music; a place for his cigarette;
Room for his knees; a honey of a clutch."

Now slowly through the show-room's flattering glare
See her wheeled in to love, console, obey,
Shining and silent! Parson with a prayer
Blesses the number-plate, she rolls away

To write her numerals in his book of life;
And now, at last, stands on the open road,
Triumphant, perfect, every inch a wife,
While the corks pop, the flash-light bulbs explode.

Her heavenly bowser-boy assumes his seat;
She prints the soft dust with her brand-new treads,
Swings towards the future, purring with a sweet
Concatenation of the poppet heads.

MOSCHUS MOSCHIFERUS

A Song for St. Cecilia's Day

In the high jungle where Assam meets Tibet
The small Kastura, most archaic of deer,
Were driven in herds to cram the hunters' net
And slaughtered for the musk-pods which they bear;

But in those thickets of rhododendron and birch
The tiny creatures now grow hard to find.
Fewer and fewer survive each year. The search
Employs new means, more exquisite and refined:

The hunters now set out by two or three;
Each carries a bow and one a slender flute.
Deep in the forest the archers choose a tree
And climb; the piper squats against the root.

And there they wait until all trace of man
And rumour of his passage dies away.
They melt into the leaves and, while they scan
The glade below, their comrade starts to play.

Through those vast listening woods a tremulous skein
Of melody wavers, delicate and shrill:
Now dancing and now pensive, now a rain
Of pure, bright drops of sound and now the still,

Sad wailing of lament; from tune to tune
It winds and modulates without a pause;
The hunters hold their breath; the trance of noon
Grows tense; with its full power the music draws

A shadow from a juniper's darker shade;
Bright-eyed, with quivering muzzle and pricked ear,
The little musk-deer slips into the glade
Led by an ecstasy that conquers fear.

A wild enchantment lures him, step by step,
Into its net of crystalline sound, until
The leaves stir overhead, the bowstrings snap
And poisoned shafts bite sharp into the kill.

Then, as the victim shudders, leaps and falls,
The music soars to a delicious peak,
And on and on its silvery piping calls
Fresh spoil for the rewards the hunters seek.

But when the woods are emptied and the dusk
Draws in, the men climb down and count their prey,
Cut out the little glands that hold the musk
And leave the carcasses to rot away.

A hundred thousand or so are killed each year;
Cause and effect are very simply linked:
Rich scents demand the musk, and so the deer,
Its source, must soon, they say, become extinct.

Divine Cecilia, there is no more to say!
Of all who praised the power of music, few
Knew of these things. In honour of your day
Accept this song that I have made for you.

W. H. AUDEN
1907-

MUSÉE DES BEAUX ARTS

About suffering they were never wrong,
The Old Masters: how well they understood
Its human position; how it takes place
While someone else is eating or opening a window or just walking
    dully along;
How, when the aged are reverently, passionately waiting
For the miraculous birth, there always must be
Children who did not specially want it to happen, skating
On a pond at the edge of the wood:
They never forgot
That even the dreadful martyrdom must run its course
Anyhow in a corner, some untidy spot
Where the dogs go on with their doggy life and the torturer's
    horse
Scratches its innocent behind on a tree.

In Brueghel's *Icarus*, for instance: how everything turns away
Quite leisurely from the disaster; the ploughman may
Have heard the splash, the forsaken cry,
But for him it was not an important failure; the sun shone
As it had to on the white legs disappearing into the green
Water; and the expensive delicate ship that must have seen
Something amazing, a boy falling out of the sky,
Had somewhere to get to and sailed calmly on.

THE UNKNOWN CITIZEN

(To JS/07/M/378 This Marble Monument Is Erected by the State)

He was found by the Bureau of Statistics to be
One against whom there was no official complaint,
And all the reports on his conduct agree
That, in the modern sense of an old-fashioned word, he was a saint,
For in everything he did he served the Greater Community.
Except for the War till the day he retired
He worked in a factory and never got fired,
But satisfied his employers, Fudge Motors Inc.
Yet he wasn't a scab or odd in his views,
For his Union reports that he paid his dues,
(Our report on his Union shows it was sound)
And our Social Psychology workers found
That he was popular with his mates and liked a drink.
The Press are convinced that he bought a paper every day
And that his reactions to advertisements were normal in every way.
Policies taken out in his name prove that he was fully insured,
And his Health-card shows he was once in hospital but left it cured.
Both Producers Research and High-Grade Living declare
He was fully sensible to the advantages of the Installment Plan
And had everything necessary to the Modern Man,
A phonograph, a radio, a car and a frigidaire.
Our researchers into Public Opinion are content
That he held the proper opinions for the time of year;
When there was peace, he was for peace; when there was war, he went.
He was married and added five children to the population,

Which our Eugenist says was the right number for a parent of his
generation,
And our teachers report that he never interfered with their educa-
tion.
Was he free? Was he happy? The question is absurd:
Had anything been wrong, we should certainly have heard.

IN MEMORY OF W. B. YEATS

I

He disappeared in the dead of winter:
The brooks were frozen, the airports almost deserted,
And snow disfigured the public statues;
The mercury sank in the mouth of the dying day.
O all the instruments agree
The day of his death was a dark cold day.

Far from his illness
The wolves ran on through the evergreen forests,
The peasant river was untempted by the fashionable quays;

By mourning tongues
The death of the poet was kept from his poems.

But for him it was his last afternoon as himself,
An afternoon of nurses and rumors;
The provinces of his body revolted,
The squares of his mind were empty,
Silence invaded the suburbs,
The current of his feeling failed: he became his admirers.

Now he is scattered among a hundred cities
And wholly given over to unfamilar affections;
To find his happiness in another kind of wood
and be punished under a foreign code of conscience.
The words of a dead man
Are modified in the guts of the living.

But in the importance and noise of tomorrow
When the brokers are roaring like beasts on the floor of the
Bourse,

And the poor have the sufferings to which they are fairly accustomed,
And each in the cell of himself is almost convinced of his freedom;
A few thousand will think of this day
As one thinks of a day when one did something slightly unusual.

O all the instruments agree
The day of his death was a dark cold day.

II

You were silly like us: your gift survived it all;
The parish of rich women, physical decay,
Yourself; mad Ireland hurt you into poetry.
Now Ireland has her madness and her weather still,
For poetry makes nothing happen: it survives
In the valley of its saying where executives
Would never want to tamper; it flows south
From ranches of isolation and the busy griefs,
Raw towns that we believe and die in; it survives,
A way of happening, a mouth.

III

Earth, receive an honored guest;
William Yeats is laid to rest:
Let the Irish vessel lie
Emptied of its poetry.

Time that is intolerant
Of the brave and innocent,
And indifferent in a week
To a beautiful physique,

Worships language and forgives
Everyone by whom it lives;

Pardons cowardice, conceit,
Lays its honors at their feet.

Time that with this strange excuse
Pardoned Kipling and his views,
And will pardon Paul Claudel,
Pardons him for writing well.

In the nightmare of the dark
All the dogs of Europe bark,
And the living nations wait,
Each sequestered in its hate;

Intellectual disgrace
Stares from every human face,
And the seas of pity lie
Locked and frozen in each eye.

Follow, poet, follow right
To the bottom of the night,
With your unconstraining voice
Still persuade us to rejoice;

With the farming of a verse
Make a vineyard of the curse,
Sing of human unsuccess
In a rapture of distress;

In the deserts of the heart
Let the healing fountain start,
In the prison of his days
Teach the free man how to praise.

THEODORE ROETHKE
1908-1963

CUTTINGS

Sticks-in-a-drowse droop over sugary loam,
Their intricate stem-fur dries;
But still the delicate slips keep coaxing up water;
The small cells bulge;

One nub of growth
Nudges a sand-crumb loose,
Pokes through a musty sheath
Its pale tendrilous horn.

CUTTINGS

(later)

This urge, wrestle, resurrection of dry sticks,
Cut stems struggling to put down feet,
What saint strained so much,
Rose on such lopped limbs to a new life?

I can hear, underground, that sucking and sobbing,
In my veins, in my bones I feel it,—
The small waters seeping upward,
The tight grains parting at last.
When sprouts break out,
Slippery as fish,
I quail, lean to beginnings, sheath-wet.

ELEGY FOR JANE

My Student, Thrown by a Horse

I remember the neckcurls, limp and damp as tendrils;
And her quick look, a sidelong pickerel smile;
And how, once startled into talk, the light syllables leaped for her,
And she balanced in the delight of her thought,
A wren, happy, tail into the wind,
Her song trembling the twigs and small branches.
The shade sang with her;
The leaves, their whispers turned to kissing;
And the mold sang in the bleached valleys under the rose.

Oh, when she was sad, she cast herself down into such a pure
depth,
Even a father could not find her:
Scraping her cheek against straw;
Stirring the clearest water.

My sparrow, you are not here,
Waiting like a fern, making a spiny shadow.
The sides of wet stones cannot console me,
Nor the moss, wound with the last light.

If I could nudge you from this sleep,
My maimed darling, my skittery pigeon.
Over this damp grave I speak the words of my love:
I, with no rights in this matter,
Neither father nor lover.

IN A DARK TIME

In a dark time, the eye begins to see,
I meet my shadow in the deepening shade;
I hear my echo in the echoing wood—
A lord of nature weeping to a tree.
I live between the heron and the wren,
Beasts of the hill and serpents of the den.

What's madness but nobility of soul
At odds with circumstance? The day's on fire!
I know the purity of pure despair,
My shadow pinned against a sweating wall.
That place among the rocks—is it a cave,
Or winding path? The edge is what I have.

A steady storm of correspondences!
A night flowing with birds, a ragged moon,
And in broad day the midnight come again!
A man goes far to find out what he is—
Death of the self in a long, tearless night,
All natural shapes blazing unnatural light.

Dark, dark my light, and darker my desire.
My soul, like some heat-maddened summer fly,
Keeps buzzing at the sill. Which I is *I?*
A fallen man, I climb out of my fear.
The mind enters itself, and God the mind,
And one is One, free in the tearing wind.

STEPHEN SPENDER
1909-

AN ELEMENTARY SCHOOL CLASSROOM IN A SLUM

Far far from gusty waves, these children's faces.
Like rootless weeds the torn hair round their paleness.
The tall girl with her weighed-down head. The paper-
seeming boy with rat's eyes. The stunted unlucky heir
Of twisted bones, reciting a father's gnarled disease,
His lesson from his desk. At back of the dim class
One unnoted, mild and young: his eyes live in a dream
Of squirrels' game, in tree room, other than this.

On sour cream walls, donations. Shakespeare's head
Cloudless at dawn, civilized dome riding all cities.
Belled, flowery, Tyrolese valley. Open-handed map
Awarding the world its world. And yet, for these
Children, these windows, not this world, are world,
Where all their future's painted with a fog,
A narrow street sealed in with a lead sky,
Far far from rivers, capes, and stars of words.

Surely Shakespeare is wicked, the map a bad example
With ships and sun and love tempting them to steal—
For lives that slyly turn in their cramped holes
From fog to endless night? On their slag heap, these children
Wear skins peeped through by bones, and spectacles of steel
With mended glass, like bottle bits in slag.
Tyrol is wicked; map's promising a fable:
All of their time and space are foggy slum,
So blot their maps with slums as big as doom.

Unless, governor, teacher, inspector, visitor,
This map becomes their window and these windows

That open on their lives like crouching tombs
Break, O break open, till they break the town
And show the children to the fields and all their world
Azure on their sands, to let their tongues
Run naked into books, the white and green leaves open
The history theirs whose language is the sun.

THE TRULY GREAT

I think continually of those who were truly great.
Who, from the womb, remembered the soul's history
Through corridors of light where the hours are suns,
Endless and singing. Whose lovely ambition
Was that their lips, still touched with fire,
Should tell of the spirit clothed from head to foot in song.
And who hoarded from the spring branches
The desires falling across their bodies like blossoms.

What is precious is never to forget
The delight of the blood drawn from ageless springs
Breaking through rocks in worlds before our earth;
Never to deny its pleasure in the simple morning light,
Nor its grave evening demand for love;
Never to allow gradually the traffic to smother
With noise and fog the flowering of the spirit.

Near the snow, near the sun, in the highest fields
See how these names are fêted by the waving grass,
And by the streamers of white cloud,
And whispers of wind in the listening sky;
The names of those who in their lives fought for life,
Who wore at their hearts the fire's center.
Born of the sun they traveled a short while towards the sun,
And left the vivid air signed with their honor.

ELIZABETH BISHOP
1911-

THE PRODIGAL

The brown enormous odor he lived by
was too close, with its breathing and thick hair,
for him to judge. The floor was rotten; the sty
was plastered halfway up with glass-smooth dung.
Light-lashed, self-righteous, above moving snouts,
the pigs' eyes followed him, a cheerful stare—
even to the sow that always ate her young—
till, sickening, he leaned to scratch her head.
But sometimes mornings after drinking bouts
(he hid the pints behind a two-by-four),
the sunrise glazed the barnyard mud with red;
the burning puddles seemed to reassure.
And then he thought he almost might endure
his exile yet another year or more.

But evenings the first star came to warn.
The farmer whom he worked for came at dark
to shut the cows and horses in the barn
beneath their overhanging clouds of hay,
with pitchforks, faint forked lightnings, catching light,
safe and companionable as in the Ark.
The pigs stuck out their little feet and snored.
The lantern—like the sun, going away—
laid on the mud a pacing aureole.
Carrying a bucket along a slimy board,
he felt the bats' uncertain staggering flight,
his shuddering insights, beyond his control,
touching him. But it took him a long time
finally to make his mind up to go home.

FLORIDA

The state with the prettiest name,
the state that floats in brackish water,
held together by mangrove roots
that bear while living oysters in clusters,
and when dead strew white swamps with skeletons,
dotted as if bombarded, with green hummocks
like ancient cannon-balls sprouting grass.
The state full of long S-shaped birds, blue and white,
and unseen hysterical birds who rush up the scale
every time in a tantrum.
Tanagers embarrassed by their flashiness,
and pelicans whose delight it is to clown;
who coast for fun on the strong tidal currents
in and out among the mangrove islands
and stand on the sand-bars drying their damp gold wings
on sun-lit evenings.
Enormous turtles, helpless and mild,
die and leave their barnacled shells on the beaches,
and their large white skulls with round eye-sockets
twice the size of a man's.
The palm trees clatter in the stiff breeze
like the bills of the pelicans. The tropical rain comes down
to freshen the tide-looped strings of fading shells:
Job's Tear, the Chinese Alphabet, the scarce Junonia,
parti-colored pectins and Ladies' Ears,
arranged as on a gray rag of rotted calico,
the buried Indian Princess's skirt;
with these the monotonous, endless, sagging coast-line
is delicately ornamented.

Thirty or more buzzards are drifting down, down, down,
over something they have spotted in the swamp,

in circles like stirred-up flakes of sediment
sinking through water.
Smoke from woods-fires filters fine blue solvents.
On stumps and dead trees the charring is like black velvet.
The mosquitoes
go hunting to the tune of their ferocious obbligatos.
After dark, the fireflies map the heavens in the marsh
until the moon rises.
Cold white, not bright, the moonlight is coarse-meshed,
and the careless, corrupt state is all black specks
too far apart, and ugly whites; the poorest
post-card of itself.
After dark, the pools seem to have slipped away.
The alligator, who has five distinct calls:
friendliness, love, mating, war, and a warning—
whimpers and speaks in the throat
of the Indian Princess.

THE ARMADILLO

This is the time of year
when almost every night
the frail, illegal fire balloons appear.
Climbing the mountain height,

rising toward a saint
still honored in these parts,
the paper chambers flush and fill with light
that comes and goes, like hearts.

Once up against the sky it's hard
to tell them from the stars—
planets, that is—the tinted ones:
Venus going down, or Mars,

or the pale green one. With a wind,
they flare and falter, wobble and toss;
but if it's still they steer between
the kite sticks of the Southern Cross,

receding, dwindling, solemnly
and steadily forsaking us,
or, in the downdraft from a peak,
suddenly turning dangerous.

Last night another big one fell.
It splattered like an egg of fire
against the cliff behind the house.
The flame ran down. We saw the pair

of owls who nest there flying up
and up, their whirling black-and-white

stained bright pink underneath, until
they shrieked up out of sight.

The ancient owls' nest must have burned.
Hastily, all alone,
a glistening armadillo left the scene,
rose-flecked, head down, tail down,

and then a baby rabbit jumped out,
short-eared, to our surprise.
So soft!—a handful of intangible ash
with fixed, ignited eyes.

Too pretty, dreamlike mimicry!
O falling fire and piercing cry
and panic, and a weak mailed fist
clenched ignorant against the sky!

MURIEL RUKEYSER
1913-

EFFORT AT SPEECH BETWEEN TWO PEOPLE

Speak to me. Take my hand. What are you now?
I will tell you all. I will conceal nothing.
When I was three, a little child read a story about a rabbit
who died, in the story, and I crawled under a chair :
a pink rabbit : it was my birthday, and a candle
burnt a sore spot on my finger, and I was told to be happy.

Oh, grow to know me. I am not happy. I will be open:
Now I am thinking of white sails against a sky like music,
like glad horns blowing, and birds tilting, and an arm about me.
There was one I loved, who wanted to live, sailing.

Speak to me. Take my hand. What are you now?
When I was nine, I was fruitily sentimental,
fluid : and my widowed aunt played Chopin,
and I bent my head to the painted woodwork, and wept.
I want now to be close to you. I would
link the minutes of my days close, somehow, to your days.

I am not happy. I will be open.
I have liked lamps in evening corners, and quiet poems.
There has been fear in my life. Sometimes I speculate on what a
    tragedy his life was, really.

Take my hand. Fist my mind in your hand. What are you
    now?
When I was fourteen, I had dreams of suicide,
I stood at a steep window, at sunset, hoping toward death :

if the light had not melted clouds and plains to beauty,
if light had not transformed that day, I would have leapt.
I am unhappy. I am lonely. Speak to me.

I will be open. I think he never loved me:
he loved the bright beaches, the little lips of foam
that ride small waves, he loved the veer of gulls:
he said with a gay mouth : I love you. Grow to know me.

What are you now? If we could touch one another,
if these our separate entities could come to grips,
clenched like a Chinese puzzle . . . yesterday
I stood in a crowded street that was live with people,
and no one spoke a word, and the morning shone.
Everyone silent, moving . . . Take my hand. Speak to me.

BOY WITH HIS HAIR CUT SHORT

Sunday shuts down on a twentieth-century evening.
The El passes. Twilight and bulb define
the brown room, the overstuffed plum sofa,
the boy, and the girl's thin hands above his head.
A neighbor radio sings stocks, news, serenade.

He sits at the table, head down, the young clear neck exposed,
watching the drugstore sign from the tail of his eye;
tattoo, neon, until the eye blears, while his
solicitous tall sister, simple in blue, bending
behind him, cuts his hair with her cheap shears.

The arrow's electric red always reaches its mark,
successful neon! He coughs, impressed by that precision.
His child's forehead, forever protected by his cap,
is bleached against the lamplight as he turns head
and steadies to let the snippets drop.

Erasing the failure of weeks with level fingers,
she sleeks the fine hair, combing : "You'll look fine tomorrow!
You'll surely find something, they can't keep turning you down;
the finest gentleman's not so trim as you!" Smiling, he raises
the adolescent forehead wrinkling ironic now.

He sees his decent suit laid out, new-pressed,
his carfare on the shelf. He lets his head fall, meeting
her earnest hopeless look, seeing the sharp blades splitting,
the darkened room, the impersonal sign, her motion,
the blue vein, bright on her temple, pitifully beating.

BRINGING

Bringing their life these young
bringing their life rise from their wakings
bringing their life come to a place
where they make their gifts

The grapes of life of death of transformation
round they hang at hand desires like peace
or seed of revolutions that make all things new
and must be lived out, washed in rivers, and themselves made new
and bringing their life the young they reach
in their griefs their mistakes their discovering
bringing their life they touch they take
bringing their life they come to a place

It is raining fire they are bringing their life
their sex speaks for them their ideas all speak
their acts arrive bringing their life entire
They resist a system of wars and rewards
They offer their open faces they offer their bodies
They offer their hands bringing their life entire
They offer their life they are their own gifts
Make life resist resist make life
Bringing their life entire they come to this moment
Bringing their life entire they come to this place

RANDALL JARRELL
1914-1965

THE DEATH OF THE BALL TURRET GUNNER

From my mother's sleep I fell into the State,
And I hunched in its belly till my wet fur froze.
Six miles from earth, loosed from its dream of life,
I woke to black flak and the nightmare fighters.
When I died they washed me out of the turret with a hose.

90 NORTH

At home, in my flannel gown, like a bear to its floe,
I clambered to bed; up the globe's impossible sides
I sailed all night—till at last, with my black beard,
My furs and my dogs, I stood at the northern pole.

There in the childish night my companions lay frozen,
The stiff furs knocked at my starveling throat,
And I gave my great sigh: the flakes came huddling,
Were they really my end? In the darkness I turned to my rest.

—Here, the flag snaps in the glare and silence
Of the unbroken ice. I stand here,
The dogs bark, my beard is black, and I stare
At the North Pole . . .
And now what? Why, go back.

Turn as I please, my step is to the south.
The world—my world spins on this final point
Of cold and wretchedness: all lines, all winds
End in this whirlpool I at last discover.

And it is meaningless. In the child's bed
After the night's voyage, in that warm world
Where people work and suffer for the end
That crowns the pain—in that Cloud-Cuckoo-Land

I reached my North and it had meaning.
Here at the actual pole of my existence,
Where all that I have done is meaningless,
Where I die or live by accident alone—

Where, living or dying, I am still alone;
Here where North, the night, the berg of death
Crowd me out of the ignorant darkness,
I see at last that all the knowledge

I wrung from the darkness—that the darkness flung me—
Is worthless as ignorance: nothing comes from nothing,
The darkness from the darkness. Pain comes from the darkness
And we call it wisdom. It is pain.

THE WOMAN AT THE WASHINGTON ZOO

The saris go by me from the embassies.

Cloth from the moon. Cloth from another planet.
They look back at the leopard like the leopard.

And I. . . .
this print of mine, that has kept its color
Alive through so many cleanings; this dull null
Navy I wear to work, and wear from work, and so
To my bed, so to my grave, with no
Complaints, no comment: neither from my chief,
The Deputy Chief Assistant, nor his chief—
Only I complain. . . . this serviceable
Body that no sunlight dyes, no hand suffuses
But, dome-shadowed, withering among columns,
Wavy beneath fountains—small, far-off, shining
In the eyes of animals, these beings trapped
As I am trapped but not, themselves, the trap,
Aging, but without knowledge of their age,
Kept safe here, knowing not of death, for death—
Oh, bars of my own body, open, open!

The world goes by my cage and never sees me.
And there come not to me, as come to these,
The wild beasts, sparrows pecking the llamas' grain,
Pigeons settling on the bears' bread, buzzards
Tearing the meat the flies have clouded. . . .
Vulture,
When you come for the white rat that the foxes left,
Take off the red helmet of your head, the black
Wings that have shadowed me, and step to me as man:
The wild brother at whose feet the white wolves fawn,

To whose hand of power the great lioness
Stalks, purring. . . .
                                        You know what I was,
You see what I am: change me, change me!

JOHN BERRYMAN
1914-1972

DREAM SONG—14

Life, friends, is boring. We must not say so.
After all, the sky flashes, the great sea yearns,
we ourselves flash and yearn,
and moreover my mother told me as a boy
(repeatingly) "Ever to confess you're bored
means you have no

Inner Resources." I conclude I have no
inner resources, because I am heavily bored.
Peoples bore me,
literature bores me, especially great literature,
Henry bores me, with his plights and gripes
as bad as Achilles,

who loves people and valiant art, which bores me.
And the tranquil hills, & gin, look like a drag
and somehow a dog
has taken itself & its tail considerably away
into mountains or sea or sky, leaving
behind: me, wag.

SONNET—60

Today is it? Is it today? I shudder
For nothing in my chair, and suddenly yawn.
Today I suddenly believe. Since dawn
When I got up, my muscles like a rudder
Strain crosswise from this work. I rise and mutter
Something, and hum, pace, and sit down again
Hard. A butterfly in my shoulder then
Stops and aches. My stomach swings like a shutter.

As the undergrounds piston a force of air
Before their crash into the station, you
Are felt before your coming, and the platforms shake.
So light, so small, so far still, to impair
Action and peace so . . . risks we take make true
Maybe our safeties . . . *come* for our risk's sake.

BARBARA HOWES
1914-

THE GALLERY

Into an empty cube
We step: the gallery,
Hung with ivory walls, lies still
As a squash court foundered in depths of sea.
Like players entering, we stare
Above the horizon line to where
Each opulent canvas, back to wall,
Confronts the room.
And then gaze on till sight
Flickers, and vision swims
In an emulsion of color, till down
Their cones of intervening air
The chipped-glass fragments form and blur.
Paintings upon four walls—nothing alive
But painting. When we have gone,
Pictures in their magnificence remain,
Tranquil as spring looking in at an open window
On an empty room.

TALKING TO ANIMALS

When there are animals about, who else—
People aside—does one talk to?
They form an environment of ear and eye
Most finely adjusted to turns
Of mood: terror, humor . . .

The domesticated: cats and dogs,
Speak freely, handle their own
Lives, adjust our natures
To theirs and back; as cattle—
Those enormous oblongs of good-

Will—did they state their strength,
Could smash a barn a day;
As ducks in their sewing circle
Wonder, wander, flapping their
Fluent tails; as a mare

Lumbers, an iron horse on the turntable,
Setting forth a fact, while her foal's eyes dance
Like legs. Smaller creatures: four
Inches of chipmunk tell hazard
From ruin as people can't . . .

Making oneself understood
To animals—as to people—
Is a question of tone of voice,
Of communication just
Right for that neighbor;

Perhaps of being inside
A hogan, or in the middle

Of anywhere, one's antennae out,
Like my Beaver-Spirit who takes—deep
In his Eskimo ear—much wisdom from a Loon.

DYLAN THOMAS
1914-1955

FERN HILL

Now as I was young and easy under the apple boughs
About the lilting house and happy as the grass was green,
    The night above the dingle starry,
        Time let me hail and climb
    Golden in the heydays of his eyes,
And honoured among wagons I was prince of the apple towns
And once below a time I lordly had the trees and leaves
        Trail with daisies and barley
    Down the rivers of the windfall light.

And as I was green and carefree, famous among the barns
About the happy yard and singing as the farm was home,
    In the sun that is young once only,
        Time let me play and be
    Golden in the mercy of his means,
And green and golden I was huntsman and herdsman, the calves
Sang to my horn, the foxes on the hills barked clear and cold,
        And the sabbath rang slowly
    In the pebbles of the holy streams.

All the sun long it was running, it was lovely, the hay
Fields high as the house, the tunes from the chimneys, it was air
    And playing, lovely and watery
        And fire green as grass.
    And nightly under the simple stars
As I rode to sleep the owls were bearing the farm away,
All the moon long I heard, blessed among stables, the nightjars
    Flying with the ricks, and the horses
        Flashing into the dark.

And then to awake, and the farm, like a wanderer white
With the dew, come back, the cock on his shoulder: it was all
        Shining, it was Adam and maiden,
                The sky gathered again
        And the sun grew round that very day.
So it must have been after the birth of the simple light
In the first, spinning place, the spellbound horses walking warm
        Out of the whinnying green stable
                On to the fields of praise.

And honoured among foxes and pheasants by the gay house
Under the new made clouds and happy as the heart was long,
        In the sun born over and over,
                I ran my heedless ways,
        My wishes raced through the house high hay
And nothing I cared, at my sky blue trades, that time allows
In all his tuneful turning so few and such morning songs
        Before the children green and golden
                Follow him out of grace,

Nothing I cared, in the lamb white days, that time would take me
Up to the swallow thronged loft by the shadow of my hand,
        In the moon that is always rising,
                Nor that riding to sleep
        I should hear him fly with the high fields
And wake to the farm forever fled from the childless land.
Oh as I was young and easy in the mercy of his means,
                Time held me green and dying
        Though I sang in my chains like the sea.

DO NOT GO GENTLE INTO THAT GOOD NIGHT

Do not go gentle into that good night,
Old age should burn and rave at close of day;
Rage, rage against the dying of the light.

Though wise men at their end know dark is right,
Because their words had forked no lightning they
Do not go gentle into that good night.

Good men, the last wave by, crying how bright
Their frail deeds might have danced in a green bay,
Rage, rage against the dying of the light.

Wild men who caught and sang the sun in flight,
And learn, too late, they grieved it on its way,
Do not go gentle into that good night.

Grave men, near death, who see with blinding sight
Blind eyes could blaze like meteors and be gay,
Rage, rage against the dying of the light.

And you, my father, there on the sad height,
Curse, bless, me now with your fierce tears, I pray.
Do not go gentle into that good night.
Rage, rage against the dying of the light.

JOHN MALCOLM BRINNIN
1916-

NUNS AT EVE

On St. Martin's evening green
Imaginary diamond, between
The vestry buttress and the convent wall,
Solemn as sea birds in a sanctuary,
Under the statue of the Virgin they play baseball.
They are all named Mary,
Sister Mary, Mary Anthony or Mary Rose,
And when the softball flies
In the shadow of the cross
The little chaplet of the Virgin's hands
Contains their soft excitements like a house.

A flying habit traces
The unprecedented rounding of the bases
By Sister Mary Agatha, who thanks God
For the easy triple and turns her eyes toward home;
As *Mary, Mother, help me* echoes in her head,
Mild cries from the proud team
Encourage her, and the obliging sun,
Dazzling the pitcher's box
With a last celestial light upon
The gold-spiked halo of the Virgin in her niche,
Leads Sister Mary John to a wild pitch.

Prayer wins the game.
As Sister Mary Agatha comes sailing home
Through infield dusk, like birds fanwise
In the vague cloisters of slow-rising mist,
Winners and losers gather in to praise
The fleetness of a bride of Christ.
Flushed and humble, Agatha collects the bats

And balls, while at her belt
Catchers' and pitchers' mitts
—Brute fingers, toes and gross lopsided heads—
Fumble the ropes of her long swinging beads.

THE ASCENSION: 1925

Step on it, said Aunt Alice, *for God's sake,*
The bloody thing is going up at four!
She crammed two broilers in a paper sack,
Harnessed the dog and pushed us out the door.
Flapping like a witch, our touring car
Ate black macadam toward Fort Frontenac
Where, trembling in her ropes, the ship of air
Rolled easy as a fifty-cent cigar.

Jesus, said Uncle Lester, *what a beaut!*
Chomping on Juicy Fruit, we eyed her close
As, nuzzling upward from her stake, she rose
In strict submission to the absolute.
We hit the highway sixty on the nose
And jettisoned our chicken bones en route.

GRAVE MIND I LOVED

Grave mind I loved, of all who mind your grave
Or lie beside, I know that John Donne's ghost
Recants the dying falls, the skull-capped love
Deaths and quick rime that—how long since!—would try
Our inarticulate mortality,
Needling for dust the flesh we favored most.

Sleep sound, sweet foundling, though I'd sound your sleep;
Make what you will of metaphysic bone,
I will not mind. Until my time is up,
Take heart, my heart, if a ghost may have one,
Have done with John's thin image and have Donne.

SKIN DIVING IN THE VIRGINS

Alfonso was his name: his sad cantina
leaned against a palm. Over my head,
he scanned a coastline only he could see
and took my order in cuneiform.

My water gear, like loose connections
from some mild machine, dripped on the table. What
a good morning! The wreck I'd shimmied through—
a sunken vessel, like Alfonso, some-
what Spanish in the stern—still weighed its gold,

while angelfish and sunfish still made mouths
to tell me nothing. That kind of poetry
one is, in principle, against. But what
sweet swarms of language to be silent in!
I tasted salt, half dreaming back and down.

All of a sudden came the pelicans:
crazy old men in baseball caps, who flew
like jackknives and collapsed like fans . . .
They'd zeroed in, Alfonso said, on fish
that shark or barracuda'd chased inshore.
Hitting the water, bull's-eye on bull's-eye,
they'd sit there rocking, naked in their smiles.

Those birds ate well.
Was there some new conclusion to be drawn
from such vast hunger without appetite?
In the next rising wave,
I saw a barracuda standing on its tail,
clear as a sea horse in a paperweight.

Alfonso, listing, brought me canned corned beef
and a cool wet Amstel winking in the bottle.
Beware of irony, I thought, and swigged my beer,
seek depths where irony cannot descend.
The bald sun rolled in the bland sky. One clown,
cartwheeling pell-mell to the kill, just missed
another floating off, his big pouch full.

GWENDOLYN BROOKS
1917-

THE RITES FOR COUSIN VIT

Carried her unprotesting out the door.
Kicked back the casket-stand. But it can't hold her,
That stuff and satin aiming to enfold her,
The lid's contrition nor the bolts before.
Oh oh. Too much. Too much. Even now, surmise,
She rises in the sunshine. There she goes,
Back to the bars she knew and the repose
In love-rooms and the things in people's eyes.
Too vital and too squeaking. Must emerge.
Even now she does the snake-hips with a hiss,
Slops the bad wine across her shantung, talks
Of pregnancy, guitars and bridgework, walks
In parks or alleys, comes haply on the verge
Of happiness, haply hysterics. Is.

MANICURE

He's betting on it this yellow mellow bit
Is buyable. Regal or Met, he'd say,
A Gordon's Dry at the Tavern. And she's got.
Her signals call. The undernourished brows.
The red fat smudge that won't make up its mind
Whether to nip nose, chin, or both together.
The face snowed under. The irresolute modesty.
Those eyes—Mayhap this chick is on the House!
To the approach. Outrageous? guy-gallant?
Paternal? frosty-with-the-heart-of-fire?
Already, this hors-d'oeuvre is in the teeth,
And all a brother has to do is bite.
Ready! . . . Aim! . . . Fire! The glass eyes break. The red
Fat moves and melts. Brows rise in lean surprise.
Bosom awakes. Maybe, she says. She might.
Well, possibly. . . . Well, call at nine tonight.

WE REAL COOL

The Pool Players.
Seven at the Golden Shovel.

We real cool. We
Left school. We

Lurk late. We
Strike straight. We

Sing sin. We
Thin gin. We

Jazz June. We
Die soon.

ROBERT LOWELL
1917-

FOR THE UNION DEAD
"Relinquunt Omnia Servare Rem Publicam."

The old South Boston Aquarium stands
in a Sahara of snow now. Its broken windows are boarded.
The bronze weathervane cod has lost half its scales.
The airy tanks are dry.

Once my nose crawled like a snail on the glass;
my hand tingled
to burst the bubbles
drifting from the noses of the cowed, compliant fish.

My hand draws back. I often sigh still
for the dark downward and vegetating kingdom
of the fish and reptile. One morning last March,
I pressed against the new barbed and galvanized

fence on the Boston Common. Behind their cage,
yellow dinosaur steamshovels were grunting
as they cropped up tons of mush and grass
to gouge their underworld garage.

Parking spaces luxuriate like civic
sandpiles in the heart of Boston.
A girdle of orange, Puritan-pumpkin colored girders
braces the tingling Statehouse,

shaking over the excavations, as it faces Colonel Shaw
and his bell-cheeked Negro infantry
on St. Gaudens' shaking Civil War relief,
propped by a plank splint against the garage's earthquake.

Two months after marching through Boston,
half the regiment was dead;
at the dedication,
William James could almost hear the bronze Negroes breathe.

Their monument sticks like a fishbone
in the city's throat.
Its Colonel is as lean
as a compass-needle.

He has an angry wrenlike vigilance,
a greyhound's gentle tautness;
he seems to wince at pleasure,
and suffocate for privacy.

He is out of bounds now. He rejoices in man's lovely,
peculiar power to choose life and die—
when he leads his black soldiers to death,
he cannot bend his back.

On a thousand small town New England greens,
the old white churches hold their air
of sparse, sincere rebellion; frayed flags
quilt the graveyards of the Grand Army of the Republic.

The stone statues of the abstract Union Soldier
grow slimmer and younger each year—
wasp-waisted, they doze over muskets
and muse through their sideburns . . .

Shaw's father wanted no monument
except the ditch,
where his son's body was thrown
and lost with his "niggers."

The ditch is nearer.
There are no statues for the last war here;
on Boylston Street, a commercial photograph
shows Hiroshima boiling

over a Mosler Safe, the "Rock of Ages"
that survived the blast. Space is nearer.
When I crouch to my television set,
the drained faces of Negro school-children rise like balloons.

Colonel Shaw
is riding on his bubble,
he waits
for the blessèd break.

The Aquarium is gone. Everywhere,
giant finned cars nose forward like fish;
a savage servility
slides by on grease.

SKUNK HOUR

Nautilus Island's hermit
heiress still lives through winter in her Spartan cottage;
her sheep still graze above the sea.
Her son's a bishop. Her farmer
is first selectman in our village;
she's in her dotage.

Thirsting for
the hierarchic privacy
of Queen Victoria's century,
she buys up all
the eyesores facing her shore,
and lets them fall.

The season's ill—
we've lost our summer millionaire,
who seemed to leap from an L. L. Bean
catalogue. His nine-knot yawl
was auctioned off to lobstermen.
A red fox stain covers Blue Hill.

And now our fairy
decorator brightens his shop for fall;
his fishnet's filled with orange cork,
orange, his cobbler's bench and awl;
there is no money in his work,
he'd rather marry.

One dark night,
my Tudor Ford climbed the hill's skull;
I watched for love-cars. Lights turned down,
they lay together, hull to hull,

where the graveyard shelves on the town. . . .
My mind's not right.

A car radio bleats,
"Love, O careless Love. . . ." I hear
my ill-spirit sob in each blood cell,
as if my hand were at its throat. . . .
I myself am hell;
nobody's here—

only skunks, that search
in the moonlight for a bite to eat.
They march on their soles up Main Street:
white stripes, moonstruck eyes' red fire
under the chalk-dry and spar spire
of the Trinitarian Church.

I stand on top
of our back steps and breathe the rich air—
a mother skunk with her column of kittens swills the garbage pail.
She jabs her wedge-head in a cup
of sour cream, drops her ostrich tail,
and will not scare.

MAN AND WIFE

Tamed by *Miltown,* we lie on Mother's bed;
the rising sun in war paint dyes us red;
in broad daylight her gilded bed-posts shine,
abandoned, almost Dionysian.
At last the trees are green on Marlborough Street,
blossoms on our magnolia ignite
the morning with their murderous five days' white.
All night I've held your hand,
as if you had
a fourth time faced the kingdom of the mad—
its hackneyed speech, its homicidal eye—
and dragged me home alive. . . . Oh my *Petite,*
clearest of all God's creatures, still all air and nerve:
you were in your twenties, and I,
once hand on glass
and heart in mouth,
outdrank the Rahvs in the heat
of Greenwich Village, fainting at your feet—
too boiled and shy
and poker-faced to make a pass,
while the shrill verve
of your invective scorched the traditional South.

Now twelve years later, you turn your back.
Sleepless, you hold
your pillow to your hollows like a child;
your old-fashioned tirade—
loving, rapid, merciless—
breaks like the Atlantic Ocean on my head.

WILLIAM JAY SMITH
1918-

REAR VISION

The cars in the mirror come swiftly forward,
While I, in thought, move slowly back;
Time past (reflected) seems to wind
Along the boundaries of mind,
A highway cold, distinct, and black.
Who knows to what the years have led,
And at which turning up ahead—
On the white-stitched road reflected back—
The furies gather in a pack,
While all the sky above burns black,
Unwinding still the darkening thread?

HULL BAY, ST. THOMAS

We come, with a busload of children, nervous from the heat,
down through lush vegetation, green from recent rain,
Down from Drake's Seat, from which the explorer must have seen
the other Virgin Islands as they are now, perched below him
in blue-green water,
Past palmetto, banana, and brown-podded flamboyant, down to
cool, yellow-brown sand under a mango tree;
And the children flee from the bus and fan out, a scattering of hot
seed, over the sand;
Come to a scene straight from an old print, black rocks jumbled
and jutting ahead into the sky,
A full red sun setting slightly to the left of the rocks, the bay
fringed with a steady surf, dark above, white beneath,
Spray flung back at the far corners of blue-black rock amid an
unravelling of pink clouds;

And all that is missing is a high-prowed frigate anchored in the
foreground, sails furled, its armored captain stepping daintily
into his boat;
The children, lost sight of like the absent frigate, find their own
abandoned boat high on the sand under the mango, and
tumble over its gun-gray gunwales like exhausted birds;
Their cries are muffled by the sound of birds sweeping through
the air, gliding slowly in, plopping on to the water,
Pelicans with ludicrous long beaks like tilted shears, or,
half-opened, like garden trowels escaped from the hands of a
mad gardener,
Pelicans circling, diving—one, two, three at a time—the silly beak
become a blade,
A surgeon's scalpel, expertly wielded, cutting through the delicate
green flesh of the water right to the fish below—

Past the snorkeler who comes up gasping for air in the agitated
water—
Beak, body, wings spelling out proudly U-O-M—as Dante saw it
written—MAN in his own language—unmistakably and
violently on the air,
While the children stare from their boat as from a Russian sleigh,
the darkening sand blown before them like snow,
The sun, askew, a blob of red quickly cut from Christmas paper,
the prow of the boat dividing nothing but the oncoming
night.

THE LIGHTNING

The lightning waked me. It slid unde r
my eyelid. A black book flipped ope n
to an illuminated page. Then insta ntly
shut. Words of destiny were being uttered in the distance. If only I could
make them out. . . . Next day as I lay
in the sun, a symbol for concei ving the
universe was scratched on my e yeball.
But quickly its point eclipse d, and
softened, in the scabbard of my brain.

My cat speaks one word. F our vowels
and a consonant. He rece ives with the
hairs of his body the wh ispers of the
stars. The kinglet spe aks by flashing
into view a ruby feath er on his head.
He is held by a threa d to the eye of the
sun, and cannot fall into error. Any
flower is a perfect ear. Or else it is
a thousand lips. . . . When will I grope my
way clear of the entrails of intellect?

TRINITY CHURCHYARD, SPRING

Thin shoulders of the old stones,
rude weathered signals of the dead,
armless and as if wearing square
robes, some with an outcrop rounded

as the head once was. Some dark
and marred as charcoal, slices broken,
are torsos rugged earth holds steady here,
perpetual in rain and wind and under

the shrill file of the years.
Some that were white have yellowed
in the sun, bent back in a stasis,
tipped by time, as candles lopped

or shortened with their use. The names
have run awry as melted wax.
Their burning has been opposite to green
and flame-shaped buds exploding now.

Gaunt remnants of one great skeleton
awaiting assembly by the church's side,
(she herself a saintly corpse
hidden in a corner of the town,

a soot-cowled ornament among the tall,
smooth-sided tombs of glass
whose ostentatious signals on the sky
heedless ask their own erasure)

their shadows grow and, longer than themselves,
repeat them on their owned and ancient grass.
Among the dead-to-be, that multiply,
huddle the frail dead undestroyed.

SUN

With your masculine stride
 you tread insidious clouds and glide
 to the unobstructed parapet of noon-blue

 ruthless rip through cumulous veils of sloth
 spurn their sly caresses and erect
 an immediate stairway to passion's splendid throne

From yourself you fling your own earth-seed
 and orbits organize in the wombless infinite
 for your discipled planets

 radiant boys
 that imitate your stamping feet
 in the elliptic dance of fire

You are not moon-dependent on desire
 in rotund rhythm leashed to a mineral despot
 like that satellite in female furrow sown

 that white rib plucked from Adam-earth
 but appended still
 eclipsed beneath his dark chest
 writhing to his will

 one-sided shield turned to the urgent tide
 compelled to yield to the night-sky slime
 she that marble-smiling sinks in moss
At dawn rubbed thin a mutilate
 she melts and faints in the cold cloud curd

while you are up afork the first ringing word
of potent joy the sharp-tined golden shout
divine and glistering your beard with dewy flames
sprinting to the pantheon and your god-like games

THE THICKENING MAT

My track the first
on new snow:
each step, with soft
snap, pressed
a padded button
into a thickening
mat—snug sensation,
satisfying pattern—
to the corner,
where I turned and

met the wind:
whips to my eyes
and mouth. This way
all I breathe
is snow. Marks
of my feet, unique,
black-edged under the
street light—
where are they?
All blank, all white.

RICHARD WILBUR
1921-

ADVICE TO A PROPHET

When you come, as you soon must, to the streets of our city,
Mad-eyed from stating the obvious,
Not proclaiming our fall but begging us
In God's name to have self-pity,

Spare us all word of the weapons, their force and range,
The long numbers that rocket the mind;
Our slow, unreckoning hearts will be left behind,
Unable to fear what is too strange.

Nor shall you scare us with talk of the death of the race.
How should we dream of this place without us?—
The sun mere fire, the leaves untroubled about us,
A stone look on the stone's face?

Speak of the world's own change. Though we cannot conceive
Of an undreamt thing, we know to our cost
How the dreamt cloud crumbles, the vines are blackened by frost,
How the view alters. We could believe,

If you told us so, that the white-tailed deer will slip
Into perfect shade, grown perfectly shy,
The lark avoid the reaches of our eye,
The jack-pine lose its knuckled grip

On the cold ledge, and every torrent burn
As Xanthus once, its gliding trout
Stunned in a twinkling. What should we be without
The dolphin's arc, the dove's return,

These things in which we have seen ourselves and spoken?
Ask us, prophet, how we shall call
Our natures forth when that live tongue is all
Dispelled, that glass obscured or broken

In which we have said the rose of our love and the clean
Horse of our courage, in which beheld
The singing locust of the soul unshelled,
And all we mean or wish to mean.

Ask us, ask us whether with the wordless rose
Our hearts shall fail us; come demanding
Whether there shall be lofty or long standing
When the bronze annals of the oak-tree close.

DIGGING FOR CHINA

"Far enough down is China," somebody said.
"Dig deep enough and you might see the sky
As clear as at the bottom of a well.
Except it would be real—a different sky.
Then you could burrow down until you came
To China! Oh, it's nothing like New Jersey.
There's people, trees, and houses, and all that,
But much, much different. Nothing looks the same."

I went and got the trowel out of the shed
And sweated like a coolie all that morning,
Digging a hole beside the lilac-bush,
Down on my hands and knees. It was a sort
Of praying, I suspect. I watched my hand
Dig deep and darker, and I tried and tried
To dream a place where nothing was the same.
The trowel never did break through to blue.

Before the dream could weary of itself
My eyes were tired of looking into darkness,
My sunbaked head of hanging down a hole.
I stood up in a place I had forgotten,
Blinking and staggering while the earth went round
And showed me silver barns, the fields dozing
In palls of brightness, patens growing and gone
In the tides of leaves, and the whole sky china blue.
Until I got my balance back again
All that I saw was China, China, China.

THE WRITER

In her room at the prow of the house
Where light breaks, and the windows are tossed with linden,
My daughter is writing a story.

I pause in the stairwell, hearing
From her shut door a commotion of typewriter-keys
Like a chain hauled over a gunwale.

Young as she is, the stuff
Of her life is a great cargo, and some of it heavy:
I wish her a lucky passage.

But now it is she who pauses,
As if to reject my thought and its easy figure.
A stillness greatens, in which

The whole house seems to be thinking,
And then she is at it again with a bunched clamor
Of strokes, and again is silent.

I remember the dazed starling
Which was trapped in that very room, two years ago;
How we stole in, lifted a sash

And retreated, not to affright it;
And how for a helpless hour, through the crack of the door,
We watched the sleek, wild, dark

And iridescent creature
Batter against the brilliance, drop like a glove
To the hard floor, or the desk-top,

And wait then, humped and bloody,
For the wits to try it again; and how our spirits
Rose when, suddenly sure,

It lifted off from a chair-back,
Beating a smooth course for the right window
And clearing the sill of the world.

It is always a matter, my darling,
Of life or death, as I had forgotten. I wish
What I wished you before, but harder.

MONA VAN DUYN
1921-

A SENTIMENTAL DELUSION

. . . There will perhaps be some men we will not love, and some machines to which we will become attached. If we find a being which looks and behaves like other men and is beyond our capacity ever to love, we must say of it that it is only a machine. . . . Should we find a machine which we can love, we must say of it that it has a human nature and human powers . . . I preserve my humanity only so far as I am one who is intrinsically able to love whatever can be loved.

Paul Weiss, "Love in a Machine Age"

WHEN our hands touched, my darling, suddenly I heard
the ticking of tinny tales, and the only words
left in the room were ours. I looked, and the hard
lights of twelve new machines turned on me and stared.
My friends, my dears, my fellow sufferers
of pulse and gland were gone. These things shed tears
in digits, only the randomizer behind their square
visages made them wander like us, but by wires.

Then, love, for a moment I was lonely. And I knew that pleasures
were up to us. We must taste for those lost others,
consider the rounded world, and kiss among pure
meters preoccupied with heat and pressure.

When, coming closer together, we walked in the streets,
my arm in yours, I heard the noise above my heartbeat
of a hundred roller-skaters, and when I let
my eyes turn from your learning look, only great
steel crates were moving around us. Those strangers in the city
buzzed through their memory banks for some clues to how we
stood, and without a click of analogy
roared by, unprogrammed for such leaning, love's oddity.

And then I understood, dear, that we two were the last
of the sweet speeders, body-snatchers, in a burst
and rush of joy before dark, before all the rest
wheel themselves coldly over our inconstant dust.

My cheek on your cheek, I could never have opened my eyes,
but I heard the whole globe rattle as it rolled in space,
its lands and waters stocked with metallic decoys.
We hold up history single-handed. But it says:
"Life has economies, and can't keep long, as guests
among stiff monsters, two yielding specialists.
Long before you die, chemistry will have you cast
from your little community of two kissing beasts."

So, love, I am afraid of love. Out of the corner of my eye
I watch for us to come uncoupled, for the dread day
when the clinch breaks, we step apart, and are free
to befriend those back to their humanity

who look at us now and see a robot pair
with sensors and effectors clamped together,
claiming our consciousness with clank and whirr,
delivering such data to each other,
that all uncoded comments lose their brightness.
Watt after watt compels us in our kiss,
and men, whose soft veins harden, envy us
our burning circuits, our immortal stress.

AN ANNUAL AND PERENNIAL PROBLEM

"Among annuals and perennials, there are not many that can properly be classed among these Heavy *and frankly seductive odors. No gardener should plant these in quantities near the house, or porch, or patio without realizing that many of them, in spite of exquisite fragrance, have a past steeped in sin."*
Taylor's Garden Guide

ONE should have known, I suppose, that you can't even trust
the lily-of-the-valley, for all it seems so chaste.

The whole lily family, in fact, is "brooding and sultry."
It's a good thing there's a Garden Guide, nothing paltry

about *their* past. Why, some are so "stinking" one expert cried,
" 'May dogs devour its hateful bulbs!' " Enough said.

We'd better not try to imagine . . . But it's hard to endure
the thought of them sitting brazenly in churches, looking pure.

The tuberose fragrance "is enhanced by dusk and becomes"
(remember, they're taken right into some people's homes,

perhaps with teen-age children around in that air!)
"intoxicating with darkness." Well, there you are.

You hear it said sometimes that in a few cases
the past can be lived down. There's no basis

for that belief—these flowers have had plenty of time.
Sinners just try to make decent folks do the same.

What we've always suspected is true. We're not safe anywhere.
Dark patios, of course— But even at our own back door

from half a block off the jasmine may try to pollute us,
and Heaven protect us all from the trailing arbutus!

HOMEWORK

Lest the fair cheeks begin their shrivelling
before a keeping eye has lit on their fairness,
I pluck from the stony world some that can't cling
to stone, for a homely, transparent form to bless.

Smothering Elbertas, if not Albertines,
in the thick, scalding sweetness of my care,
I add a touch of tart malice, some spicy scenes
and stirring, and screw the lid on love's breathless jar.

There in a frieze they stand, and there they can stay
until, in the fickle world's or the jaded heart's
hunger for freshness, they are consumed away.
Oh I know, I know that, great or humble, the arts

in their helplessness can save but a few selves
by such disguises from Time's hideous bite,
and yet, a sweating Proust of the pantry shelves,
I cupboard these pickled peaches in Time's despite.

JAMES DICKEY
1923-

THE FIREBOMBING

Denke daran, dass nach den grossen
    Zerstörungen
Jedermann beweisen wird, dass er
    unshuldig war.

—Günter Eich

Or hast thou an arm like God?

—The Book of Job

Homeowners unite.

All families lie together, though some are burned alive.
The others try to feel
For them. Some can, it is often said.

Starve and take off

Twenty years in the suburbs, and the palm trees willingly leap
Into the flashlights,
And there is beneath them also
A booted crackling of snailshells and coral sticks.
There are cowl flaps and the tilt cross of propellers,
The shovel-marked clouds' far sides against the moon,
The enemy filling up the hills
With ceremonial graves. At my somewhere among these,

Snap, a bulb is tricked on in the cockpit

And some technical-minded stranger with my hands
Is sitting in a glass treasure-hole of blue light,
Having potential fire under the undeodorized arms
Of his wings, on thin bomb-shackles,

The "tear-drop-shaped" 300-gallon drop-tanks
Filled with napalm and gasoline.

Thinking forward ten minutes
From that, there is also the burst straight out
Of the overcast into the moon; there is now
The moon-metal-shine of propellers, the quarter-
moonstone, aimed at the waves,
Stopped on the cumulus.

There is then this re-entry
Into cloud, for the engines to ponder their sound.
In white dark the aircraft shrinks; Japan

Dilates around it like a thought.
Coming out, the one who is here is over
Land, passing over the all-night grainfields,
In dark paint over
The woods with one silver side,
Rice-water calm at all levels
Of the terraced hill.
                                        Enemy rivers and trees
Sliding off me like snakeskin,
Strips of vapor spooled from the wingtips
Going   invisible   passing   over   on
Over   bridges   roads for nightwalkers
Sunday night in the enemy's country   absolute
Calm   the moon's face   coming   slowly
About
            the inland sea
Slants   is woven with wire thread
Levels out   holds together like a quilt
Off the starboard wing   cloud flickers
At my glassed-off forehead   the moon's now and again

Uninterrupted face going forward
Over the waves in a glide-path
Lost into land.

Going: going with it

Combat booze by my side in a cratered canteen,
Bourbon frighteningly mixed
With GI pineapple juice,
Dogs trembling under me for hundreds of miles, on many
Islands, sleep-smelling that ungodly mixture
Of napalm and high-octane fuel,
Good bourbon and GI juice.

Rivers circling behind me around
Come to the fore, and bring
A town with everyone darkened.
Five thousand people are sleeping off
An all-day American drone.
Twenty years in the suburbs have not shown me
Which ones were hit and which not.

Haul on the wheel   racking slowly
The aircraft blackly around
In a dark dream   that   that is
That is like flying inside someone's head

Think of this   think of this

I did not think of my house
But think of my house now

Where the lawnmower rests on its laurels
Where the diet exists

For my own good   where I try to drop
Twenty years, eating figs in the pantry
Blinded by each and all
Of the eye-catching cans that gladly have caught my wife's eye
Until I cannot say
Where the screwdriver is   where the children
Get off the bus   where the new
Scoutmaster lives   where the fly
Hones his front legs   where the hammock folds
Its erotic daydreams   where the Sunday
School text for the day has been put   where the fire
Wood is   where the payments
For everything under the sun
Pile peacefully up,

But in this half-paid-for pantry
Among the red lids that screw off
With an easy half-twist to the left
And the long drawers crammed with dim spoons,
I still have charge—secret charge—
Of the fire developed to cling
To everything: to golf carts and fingernail
Scissors as yet unborn   tennis shoes
Grocery baskets   toy fire engines
New Buicks stalled by the half-moon
Shining at midnight on crossroads   green paint
Of jolly garden tools   red Christmas ribbons:

Not atoms, these, but glue inspired
By love of country to burn,
The apotheosis of gelatin.

Behind me having risen the Southern Cross
Set up by chaplains in the Ryukyus—

Orion, Scorpio, the immortal silver
Like the myths of king-
insects at swarming time—
One mosquito, dead drunk
On altitude, drones on, far under the engines,
And bites between
The oxygen mask and the eye.
The enemy-colored skin of families
Determines to hold its color
In sleep, as my hand turns whiter
Than ever, clutching the toggle—
The ship shakes   bucks
Fire hangs   not yet fire
In the air above Beppu
For I am fulfilling

An "anti-morale" raid upon it.
All leashes of dogs
Break under the first bomb, around those
In bed, or late in the public baths: around those
Who inch forward on their hands
Into medicinal waters.
Their heads come up with a roar
Of Chicago fire:
Come up with the carp pond showing
The bathhouse upside down,
Standing stiller to show it more
As I sail artistically over
The resort town followed by farms,
Singing and twisting
All the handles in heaven   kicking
The small cattle off their feet
In a red costly blast
Flinging jelly over the walls

As in a chemical war-
fare field demonstration.
With fire of mine like a cat

Holding onto another man's walls,
My hat should crawl on my head
In streetcars, thinking of it,
The fat on my body should pale.

Gun down
The engines, the eight blades sighing
For the moment when the roofs will connect
Their flames, and make a town burning with all
American fire.
                Reflections of houses catch;
Fire shuttles from pond to pond
In every direction, till hundreds flash with one death.
With this in the dark of the mind,
Death will not be what it should;
Will not, even now, even when
My exhaled face in the mirror
Of bars, dilates in a cloud like Japan.
The death of children is ponds
Shutter-flashing; responding mirrors; it climbs
The terraces of hills
Smaller and smaller, a mote of red dust
At a hundred feet; at a hundred and one it goes out.
That is what should have got in
To my eye
And shown the insides of houses, the low tables
Catch fire from the floor mats,
Blaze up in gas around their heads
Like a dream of suddenly growing
Too intense for war. Ah, under one's dark arms

Something strange-scented falls—when those on earth
Die, there is not even sound;
One is cool and enthralled in the cockpit,
Turned blue by the power of beauty,
In a pale treasure-hole of soft light
Deep in aesthetic contemplation,
Seeing the ponds catch fire
And cast it through ring after ring
Of land: O death in the middle
Of acres of inch-deep water!   Useless

Firing   small arms
Speckles   from the river
Bank   one ninety-millimeter
Misses   far down   wrong petals   gone

It is this detachment,
The honored aesthetic evil,
The greatest sense of power in one's life,
That must be shed in bars, or by whatever
Means, by starvation
Visions in well-stocked pantries:
The moment when the moon sails in between
The tail-booms   the rudders nod   I swing
Over   directly over the heart
The *heart* of the fire. A mosquito burns out on my cheek
With the cold of my face   there are the eyes
In blue light   bar light
All masked but them   the moon
Crossing from left to right   in the streams below
Oriental fish form quickly
In the chemical shine,
In their eyes one tiny seed
Of deranged, Old Testament light.

Letting go   letting go
The plane rises gently   dark forms
Glide off me   long water   pales
In safe zones   a new cry enters
The voice box of chained family dogs

We buck   leap over something
Not there   settle back
Leave it   leave it clinging and crying
It consumes them in a hot
Body-flash, old age or menopause
Of children, clings and burns
                                        eating through
And when a reed mat catches fire
From me, it explodes through field after field
Bearing its sleeper   another

Bomb finds a home
And clings to it like a child. And so

Goodbye to the grassy mountains
To cloud streaming from the night engines
Flags   pennons   curved silks
Of air   myself streaming also
My body covered
With flags, the air of flags
Between the engines.
Forever I do sleep in that position,
Forever in a turn
For home that breaks out streaming banners
From my wingtips,
Wholly in position to admire.

O then I knock it off

And turn for home over the black complex thread worked
    through
The silver night-sea,
Following the huge, moon-washed steppingstones
Of the Ryukyus south,
The nightgrass of mountains billowing softly

In my rising heat.
                              Turn and tread down
The yellow stones of the islands
To where Okinawa burns,
Pure gold, on the radar screen,
Beholding, beneath, the actual island form
In the vast water-silver poured just above solid ground,
An inch of water extending for thousands of miles
Above flat ploughland. Say "down," and it is done.

All this, and I am still hungry,
Still twenty years overweight, still unable
To get down there or see
What really happened.
                              But it may be that I could not,
If I tried, say to any
Who lived there, deep in my flames: say, in cold
Grinning sweat, as to another
As these homeowners who are always curving
Near me down the different-grassed street: say
As though to the neighbor
I borrowed the hedge-clippers from
On the darker-grassed side of the two,
Come in, my house is yours, come in
If you can, if you
Can pass this unfired door. It is that I can imagine
At the threshold nothing

With its ears crackling off
Like powdery leaves,
Nothing with children of ashes, nothing not
Amiable, gentle, well-meaning,
A little nervous for no
Reason   a little worried   a little too loud
Or too easygoing   nothing I haven't lived with
For twenty years, still nothing not as
American as I am, and proud of it.

Absolution? Sentence? No matter;
The thing itself is in that.

LOUIS SIMPSON
1923-

THINGS

A man stood in the laurel tree
Adjusting his hands and feet to the boughs.
He said, "Today I was breaking stones
On a mountain road in Asia,

When suddenly I had a vision
Of mankind, like grass and flowers,
The same over all the earth.
We forgave each other; we gave ourselves
Wholly over to words.
And straightway I was released
And sprang through an open gate."

I said, "Into a meadow?"

He said, "I am impervious to irony.
I thank you for the word. . . .
I am standing in a sunlit meadow.
Know that everything your senses reject
Springs up in the spiritual world."

I said, "Our scientists have another opinion.
They say, you are merely phenomena."

He said, "Over here they will be angels
Singing, Holy holy be His Name!
And also, it works in reverse.
Things which to us in the pure state are mysterious,
Are your simplest articles of household use—
A chair, a dish, and meaner even than these,
The very latest inventions.

Machines are the animals of the Americans—
Tell me about machines."

I said, "I have suspected
The Mixmaster knows more than I do,
The air conditioner is the better poet.
My right front tire is as bald as Odysseus—
How much it must have suffered!

Then, as things have a third substance
Which is obscure to both our senses,
Let there be a perpetual coming and going
Between your house and mine."

AFTER MIDNIGHT

The dark streets are deserted,
With only a drugstore glowing
Softly, like a sleeping body;

With one white, naked bulb
In the back, that shines
On suicides and abortions.

Who lives in these dark houses?
I am suddenly aware
I might live here myself.

The garage man returns
And puts the change in my hand,
Counting the singles carefully.

MASHKIN HILL

When Levin mowed Mashkin Hill
there were moments of happy self-forgetfulness.
When he talked to a peasant who believed in God,
Levin realized that he too believed.

In the modern world there aren't any peasants.
They don't cut hay with a scythe,
or the women rake it in windrows.
Now all that work is done by machines.

Now the farmer comes home like anyone
to find that his wife has had her hair done,
and that they're dining by candlelight,
the children having been fed.

And there is no God for Levin
but the quietness of his house.

SAMUEL SEWALL

Samuel Sewall, in a world of wigs,
Flouted opinion in his personal hair;
For foppery he gave not any figs,
But in his right and honor took the air.

Thus in his naked style, though well attired,
He went forth in the city, or paid court
To Madam Winthrop, whom he much admired,
Most Godly, but yet liberal with the port.

And all the town admired for two full years
His excellent address, his gifts of fruit,
Her gracious ways and delicate white ears,
And held the course of nature absolute.

But yet she bade him suffer a peruke,
"That One be not distinguished from the All";
Delivered of herself this stern rebuke
Framed in the resonant language of St. Paul.

"Madam," he answered her, "I have a Friend
Furnishes me with hair out of His strength,
And He requires only I attend
Unto His charity and to its length."

And all the town was witness to his trust:
On Monday he walked out with the Widow Gibbs,
A pious lady of charm and notable bust,
Whose heart beat tolerably beneath her ribs.

On Saturday he wrote proposing marriage,
And closed, imploring that she be not cruel,
"Your favorable answer will oblige,
Madam, your humble servant, Samuel Sewall."

"IT OUT-HERODS HEROD. PRAY YOU, AVOID IT."

Tonight my children hunch
Toward their Western, and are glad
As, with a Sunday punch,
The Good casts out the Bad.

And in their fairy tales
The warty giant and witch
Get sealed in doorless jails
And the match-girl strikes it rich.

I've made myself a drink.
The giant and witch are set
To bust out of the clink
When my children have gone to bed.

All frequencies are loud
With signals of despair;
In flash and morse they crowd
The rondure of the air.

For the wicked have grown strong,
Their numbers mock at death,
Their cow brings forth its young,
Their bull engendereth.

Their very fund of strength,
Satan, bestrides the globe;
He stalks its breadth and length
And finds out even Job.

Yet by quite other laws
My children make their case;
Half God, half Santa Claus,
But with my voice and face,

A hero comes to save
The poorman, beggarman, thief,
And make the world behave
And put an end to grief.

And that their sleep be sound
I say this childermas
Who could not, at one time,
Have saved them from the gas.

MORE LIGHT! MORE LIGHT!

Composed in the Tower before his execution
These moving verses, and being brought at that time
Painfully to the stake, submitted, declaring thus:
"I implore my God to witness that I have made no crime."

Nor was he forsaken of courage, but the death was horrible,
The sack of gunpowder failing to ignite.
His legs were blistered sticks on which the black sap
Bubbled and burst as he howled for the Kindly Light.

And that was but one, and by no means one of the worst;
Permitted at least his pitiful dignity;
And such as were by made prayers in the name of Christ,
That shall judge all men, for his soul's tranquillity.

We move now to outside a German wood.
Three men are there commanded to dig a hole
In which the two Jews are ordered to lie down
And be buried alive by the third, who is a Pole.

Not light from the shrine at Weimar beyond the hill
Nor light from heaven appeared. But he did refuse. A Lüger settled back deeply in its glove.
He was ordered to change places with the Jews.

Much casual death had drained away their souls.
The thick dirt mounted toward the quivering chin.
When only the head was exposed the order came
To dig him out again and to get back in.

No light, no light in the blue Polish eye.
When he finished a riding boot packed down the earth.

The Lüger hovered lightly in its glove.
He was shot in the belly and in three hours bled to death.

No prayers or incense rose up in those hours
Which grew to be years, and every day came mute
Ghosts from the ovens, sifting through crisp air,
And settled upon his eyes in a black soot.

W. D. SNODGRASS
1926-

APRIL INVENTORY

The green catalpa tree has turned
All white; the cherry blooms once more.
In one whole year I haven't learned
A blessed thing they pay you for.
The blossoms snow down in my hair;
The trees and I will soon be bare.

The trees have more than I to spare.
The sleek, expensive girls I teach,
Younger and pinker every year,
Bloom gradually out of reach.
The pear tree lets its petals drop
Like dandruff on a tabletop.

The girls have grown so young by now
I have to nudge myself to stare.
This year they smile and mind me how
My teeth are falling with my hair.
In thirty years I may not get
Younger, shrewder, or out of debt.

The tenth time, just a year ago,
I made myself a little list
Of all the things I'd ought to know,
Then told my parents, analyst,
And everyone who's trusted me
I'd be substantial, presently.

I haven't read one book about
A book or memorized one plot.
Or found a mind I did not doubt.

I learned one date. And then forgot.
And one by one the solid scholars
Get the degrees, the jobs, the dollars.

And smile above their starchy collars.
I taught my classes Whitehead's notions;
One lovely girl, a song of Mahler's.
Lacking a source-book or promotions,
I showed one child the colors of
A luna moth and how to love.

I taught myself to name my name,
To bark back, loosen love and crying;
To ease my woman so she came,
To ease an old man who was dying.
I have not learned how often I
Can win, can love, but choose to die.

I have not learned there is a lie
Love shall be blonder, slimmer, younger;
That my equivocating eye
Loves only by my body's hunger;
That I have forces, true to feel,
Or that the lovely world is real.

While scholars speak authority
And wear their ulcers on their sleeves,
My eyes in spectacles shall see
These trees procure and spend their leaves.
There is a value underneath
The gold and silver in my teeth.

Though trees turn bare and girls turn wives,
We shall afford our costly seasons;

There is a gentleness survives
That will outspeak and has its reasons.
There is a loveliness exists,
Preserves us, not for specialists.

MEMENTOS, 1

Sorting out letters and piles of my old
  Canceled checks, old clippings, and yellow note cards
That meant something once, I happened to find
  Your picture. *That* picture. I stopped there cold,
Like a man raking piles of dead leaves in his yard
    Who has turned up a severed hand.

Still, that first second, I was glad: you stand
  Just as you stood—shy, delicate, slender,
In that long gown of green lace netting and daisies
  That you wore to our first dance. The sight of you stunned
Us all. Well, our needs were different, then,
    And our ideals came easy.

Then through the war and those two long years
  Overseas, the Japanese dead in their shacks
Among dishes, dolls, and lost shoes; I carried
  This glimpse of you, there, to choke down my fear,
Prove it has been, that it might come back.
    That was before we got married.

—Before we drained out one another's force
  With lies, self-denial, unspoken regret
And the sick eyes that blame; Before the divorce
  And the treachery. Say it: before we met. Still,
I put back your picture. Someday, in due course,
    I will find that it's still there.

WHAT WE SAID

Stunned in that first estrangement,
We went through the turning woods
Where inflamed leaves sick as words
Spun, wondering what the change meant.

Half gone, our road led onwards
By barbed wire, past the ravine
Where a lost couch, snarled in veins,
Spilled its soiled, gray innards

Into a garbage mound.
We came, then, to a yard
Where tarpaper, bottles and charred
Boards lay on the trampled ground.

This had been someone's lawn.
And, closing up like a wound,
The cluttered hole in the ground
A life had been built upon.

In the high grass, cars had been.
On the leafless branches, rags
And condoms fluttered like the flags
Of new orders moving in.

We talked of the last war, when
Houses, cathedral towns, shacks—
Whole continents went into wreckage.
What fools could do that again?

Ruin on every side—
We would set our loves in order,
Surely, we told each other.
Surely. That's what we said.

ALLEN GINSBERG
1926-

From "KADDISH"

For Naomi Ginsberg 1894–1956

I

Strange now to think of you, gone without corsets & eyes, while I walk on the sunny pavement of Greenwich Village.
downtown Manhattan, clear winter noon, and I've been up all night, talking, talking, reading the Kaddish aloud, listening to Ray Charles blues shout blind on the phonograph
the rhythm the rhythm—and your memory in my head three years after—And read Adonais' last triumphant stanzas aloud—wept, realizing how we suffer—
And how Death is that remedy all singers dream of, sing, remember, prophesy as in the Hebrew Anthem, or the Buddhist Book of Answers—and my own imagination of a withered leaf—at dawn—
Dreaming back thru life, Your time—and mine accelerating toward Apocalypse,
the final moment—the flower burning in the Day—and what comes after,
looking back on the mind itself that saw an American city
a flash away, and the great dream of Me or China, or you and a phantom Russia, or a crumpled bed that never existed—
like a poem in the dark—escaped back to Oblivion—
No more to say, and nothing to weep for but the Beings in the Dream, trapped in its disappearance,
sighing, screaming with it, buying and selling pieces of phantom, worshipping each other,
worshipping the God included in it all—longing or inevitability? —while it lasts, a Vision—anything more?
It leaps about me, as I go out and walk the street, look back over my shoulder, Seventh Avenue, the battlements of window

office buildings shouldering each other high, under a cloud, tall as the sky an instant—and the sky above—an old blue place.
or down the Avenue to the South, to—I walk toward the Lower East Side—where you walked 50 years ago, little girl—from Russia, eating the first poisonous tomatoes of America—frightened on the dock—
then struggling in the crowds of Orchard Street toward what?—toward Newark—
toward candy store, first home-made sodas of the century, hand-churned ice cream in backroom on musty brownfloor boards—
Toward education marriage nervous breakdown, operation, teaching school, and learning to be mad, in a dream—what is this life?
Toward the Key in the window—and the great Key lays its head of light on top of Manhattan, and over the floor, and lays down on the sidewalk—in a single vast beam, moving, as I walk down First toward the Yiddish Theater—and the place of poverty
you knew, and I know, but without caring now—Strange to have moved thru Paterson, and the West, and Europe and here again,
with the cries of Spaniards now in the doorstoops doors and dark boys on the street, fire escapes old as you
—Tho you're not old now, that's left here with me—
Myself, anyhow, maybe as old as the universe—and I guess that dies with us—enough to cancel all that comes—What came is gone forever every time—
That's good! That leaves it open for no regret—no fear radiators, lacklove, torture even toothache in the end—
Though while it comes it is a lion that eats the soul—and the lamb, the soul, in us, alas, offering itself in sacrifice to

change's fierce hunger—hair and teeth—and the roar of bonepain, skull bare, break rib, rot-skin, braintricked Implacability.

Ai! ai! we do worse! We are in a fix! And you're out, Death let you out, Death had the Mercy, you're done with your century, done with God, done with the path thru it—Done with yourself at last—Pure—Back to the Babe dark before your Father, before us all—before the world—

There, rest. No more suffering for you. I know where you've gone, it's good . . .

A SUPERMARKET IN CALIFORNIA

What thoughts I have of you tonight, Walt Whitman, for I walked down the sidestreets under the trees with a headache self-conscious looking at the full moon.

In my hungry fatigue, and shopping for images, I went into the neon fruit supermarket, dreaming of your enumerations!

What peaches and what penumbras! Whole families shopping at night! Aisles full of husbands! Wives in the avocados, babies in the tomatoes!—and you, Garcia Lorca, what were you doing down by the watermelons?

I saw you, Walt Whitman, childless, lonely old grubber, poking among the meats in the refrigerator and eyeing the grocery boys.

I heard you asking questions of each: Who killed the pork chops? What price bananas? Are you my Angel?

I wandered in and out of the brilliant stacks of cans following you, and followed in my imagination by the store detective.

We strode down the open corridors together in our solitary fancy tasting artichokes, possessing every frozen delicacy, and never passing the cashier.

Where are we going, Walt Whitman? The doors close in an hour. Which way does your beard point tonight?

(I touch your book and dream of our odyssey in the supermarket and feel absurd.)

Will we walk all night through solitary streets? The trees add shade to shade, lights out in the houses, we'll both be lonely.

Will we stroll dreaming of the lost America of love past

blue automobiles in driveways, home to our silent cottage?

Ah, dear father, graybeard, lonely old courage-teacher, what America did you have when Charon quit poling his ferry and you got out on a smoking bank and stood watching the boat disappear on the black waters of Lethe?

W. S. MERWIN
1927-

THE DRUNK IN THE FURNACE

For a good decade
The furnace stood in the naked gully, fireless
And vacant as any hat. Then when it was
No more to them than a hulking black fossil
To erode unnoticed with the rest of the junk-hill
By the poisonous creek, and rapidly to be added
To their ignorance.

They were afterwards astonished
To confirm, one morning, a twist of smoke like a pale
Resurrection, staggering out of its chewed hole,
And to remark then other tokens that someone,
Cosily bolted behind the eye-holed iron
Door of the drafty burner, had there established
His bad castle.

Where he gets his spirits
It's a mystery. But the stuff keeps him musical:
Hammer-and-anvilling with poker and bottle
To his jugged bellowings, till the last groaning clang
As he collapses onto the rioting
Springs of a litter of car-seats ranged on the grates,
To sleep like an iron pig.

In their tar-paper church
On a text about stoke-holes that are sated never
Their Reverend lingers. They nod and hate trespassers.
When the furnace wakes, though, all afternoon
Their witless offspring flock like piped rats to its siren
Crescendo, and agape on the crumbling ridge
Stand in a row and learn.

SMALL WOMAN ON SWALLOW STREET

Four feet up, under the bruise-blue
Fingered hat-felt, the eyes begin. The sly brim
Slips over the sky, street after street, and nobody
Knows, to stop it. It will cover
The whole world, if there is time. Fifty years'
Start in gray the eyes have; you will never
Catch up to where they are, too clever
And always walking, the legs not long but
The boots big with wide smiles of darkness
Going round and round at their tops, climbing.
They are almost to the knees already, where
There should have been ankles to stop them.
So must keep walking all the time, hurry, for
The black sea is down where the toes are
And swallows and swallows all. A big coat
Can help save you. But eyes push you down; never
Meet eyes. There are hands in hands, and love
Follows its furs into shut doors; who
Shall be killed first? Do not look up there:
The wind is blowing the building-tops, and a hand
Is sneaking the whole sky another way, but
It will not escape. Do not look up. God is
On High. He can see you. You will die.

WESTERN COUNTRY

Some days after so long even the sun
is foreign
I watch the exiles
their stride
stayed by their antique faith that no one
can die in exile
when all that is true is that death is not exile

Each no doubt knows a western country
half discovered
which he thinks is there because
he thinks he left it
and its names are still written in the sun
in his age and he knows them
but he will never tread their ground

At some distances I can no longer
sleep
my countrymen are more cruel than their stars
and I know what moves the long
files stretching into the mountains
each man with his gun
his feet
one finger's breadth off the ground

GALWAY KINNELL
1927-

THE BEAR

I

In late winter
I sometimes glimpse bits of steam
coming up from
some fault in the old snow
and bend close and see it is lung-colored
and put down my nose
and know
the chilly, enduring odor of bear.

II

I take a wolf's rib and whittle
it sharp at both ends
and coil it up
and freeze it in blubber and place it out
on the fairway of the bears.

And when it has vanished
I move out on the bear tracks,
roaming in circles
until I come to the first, tentative, dark
splash on the earth.

And I set out
running, following the splashes
of blood wandering over the world.
At the cut, gashed resting places
I stop and rest,
at the crawl-marks
where he lay out on his belly
to overpass some stretch of bauchy ice

I lie out
dragging myself forward with bear-knives in my fists.

III

On the third day I begin to starve,
at nightfall I bend down as I knew I would
at a turd sopped in blood,
and hesitate, and pick it up,
and thrust it in my mouth, and gnash it down,
and rise
and go on running.

IV

On the seventh day,
living by now on bear blood alone,
I can see his upturned carcass far out ahead, a scraggled,
steamy hulk,
the heavy fur riffling in the wind.

I come up to him
and stare at the narrow-spaced, petty eyes,
the dismayed
face laid back on the shoulder, the nostrils
flared, catching
perhaps the first taint of me as he
died.

I hack
a ravine in his thigh, and eat and drink,
and tear him down his whole length
and open him and climb in
and close him up after me, against the wind,
and sleep.

V

And dream
of lumbering flatfooted
over the tundra,
stabbed twice from within,
splattering a trail behind me,
splattering it out no matter which way I lurch,
no matter which parabola of bear-transcendence,
which dance of solitude I attempt,
which gravity-clutched leap,
which trudge, which groan.

VI

Until one day I totter and fall—
fall on this
stomach that has tried so hard to keep up,
to digest the blood as it leaked in,
to break up
and digest the bone itself: and now the breeze
blows over me, blows off
the hideous belches of ill-digested bear blood
and rotted stomach
and the ordinary, wretched odor of bear,

blows across
my sore, lolled tongue a song
or screech, until I think I must rise up
and dance. And I lie still.

VII

I awaken I think. Marshlights
reappear, geese
come trailing again up the flyway.
In her ravine under old snow the dam-bear

lies, licking
lumps of smeared fur
and drizzly eyes into shapes
with her tongue. And one
hairy-soled trudge stuck out before me,
the next groaned out,
the next,
the next,
the rest of my days I spend
wandering: wondering
what, anyway,
was that sticky infusion, that rank flavor of blood, that poetry, by
which I lived?

VAPOR TRAIL REFLECTED IN THE FROG POND

I

The old watch: their
thick eyes
puff and foreclose by the moon. The young, heads
trailed by the beginnings of necks,
shiver,
in the guarantee they shall be bodies.

In the frog pond
the vapor trail of a SAC bomber creeps,

I hear its drone, drifting, high up
in immaculate ozone.

II

And I hear,
coming over the hills, America singing,
her varied carols I hear:
crack of deputies' rifles practicing their aim on stray dogs at night,
sput of cattleprod,
TV groaning at the smells of the human body,
curses of the soldier as he poisons, burns, grinds, and stabs
the rice of the world,
with open mouth, crying strong, hysterical curses.

III

And by rice paddies in Asia
bones
wearing a few shadows
walk down a dirt road, smashed
bloodsuckers on their heel, knowing

the flesh a man throws down in the sunshine
dogs shall eat
and the flesh that is upthrown in the air
shall be seized by birds,
shoulder blades smooth, unmarked by old feather-holes,
hands rivered
by blue, erratic wanderings of the blood,
eyes crinkled up
as they gaze up at the drifting sun that gives us our lives,
seed dazzled over the footbattered blaze of the earth.

SOME TREES

These are amazing: each
Joining a neighbor, as though speech
Were a still performance.
Arranging by chance

To meet as far this morning
From the world as agreeing
With it, you and I
Are suddenly what the trees try

To tell us we are:
That their merely being there
Means something; that soon
We may touch, love, explain.

And glad not to have invented
Such comeliness, we are surrounded:
A silence already filled with noises,
A canvas on which emerges

A chorus of smiles, a winter morning.
Placed in a puzzling light, and moving,
Our days put on such reticence
These accents seem their own defense.

THE PAINTER

Sitting between the sea and the buildings
He enjoyed painting the sea's portrait.
But just as children imagine a prayer
Is merely silence, he expected his subject
To rush up the sand, and, seizing a brush,
Plaster its own portrait on the canvas.

So there was never any paint on his canvas
Until the people who lived in the buildings
Put him to work: "Try using the brush
As a means to an end. Select, for a portrait,
Something less angry and large, and more subject
To a painter's moods, or, perhaps, to a prayer."

How could he explain to them his prayer
That nature, not art, might usurp the canvas?
He chose his wife for a new subject,
Making her vast, like ruined buildings,
As if, forgetting itself, the portrait
Had expressed itself without a brush.

Slightly encouraged, he dipped his brush
In the sea, murmuring a heartfelt prayer:
"My soul, when I paint this next portrait
Let it be you who wrecks the canvas."
The news spread like wildfire through the buildings:
He had gone back to the sea for his subject.

Imagine a painter crucified by his subject!
Too exhausted even to lift his brush,
He provoked some artists leaning from the buildings
To malicious mirth: "We haven't a prayer

Now, of putting ourselves on canvas,
Or getting the sea to sit for a portrait!"

Others declared it a self-portrait.
Finally all indications of a subject
Began to fade, leaving the canvas
Perfectly white. He put down the brush.
At once a howl, that was also a prayer,
Arose from the overcrowded buildings.

They tossed him, the portrait, from the tallest of the buildings;
And the sea devoured the canvas and the brush
As if his subject had decided to remain a prayer.

JAMES WRIGHT
1927-

A BLESSING

Just off the highway to Rochester, Minnesota,
Twilight bounds softly forth on the grass.
And the eyes of those two Indian ponies
Darken with kindness.
They have come gladly out of the willows
To welcome my friend and me.
We step over the barbed wire into the pasture
Where they have been grazing all day, alone.
They ripple tensely, they can hardly contain their happiness
That we have come.
They bow shyly as wet swans. They love each other.
There is no loneliness like theirs.
At home once more,
They begin munching the young tufts of spring in the darkness.
I would like to hold the slenderer one in my arms,
For she has walked over to me
And nuzzled my left hand.
She is black and white,
Her mane falls wild on her forehead,
And the light breeze moves me to caress her long ear
That is delicate as the skin over a girl's wrist.
Suddenly I realize
That if I stepped out of my body I would break
Into blossom.

BEGINNING

The moon drops one or two feathers into the field.
The dark wheat listens.
Be still.
Now.
There they are, the moon's young, trying
Their wings.
Between trees, a slender woman lifts up the lovely shadow
Of her face, and now she steps into the air, now she is gone
Wholly, into the air.
I stand alone by an elder tree, I do not dare breathe
Or move.
I listen.
The wheat leans back toward its own darkness,
And I lean toward mine.

MARY BLY

I sit here, doing nothing, alone, worn out by long winter.
I feel the light breath of the newborn child.
Her face is smooth as the side of an apricot,
Eyes quick as her blond mother's hands.
She has full, soft, red hair, and as she lies quiet
In her tall mother's arms, her delicate hands
Weave back and forth.
I feel the seasons changing beneath me,
Under the floor.
She is braiding the waters of air into the plaited manes
Of happy colts.
They canter, without making a sound, along the shores
Of melting snow.

ANNE SEXTON
1928-

YOU, DOCTOR MARTIN

You, Doctor Martin, walk
from breakfast to madness. Late August,
I speed through the antiseptic tunnel
where the moving dead still talk
of pushing their bones against the thrust
of cure. And I am queen of this summer hotel
or the laughing bee on a stalk

of death. We stand in broken
lines and wait while they unlock
the door and count us at the frozen gates
of dinner. The shibboleth is spoken
and we move to gravy in our smock
of smiles. We chew in rows, our plates
scratch and whine like chalk

in school. There are no knives
for cutting your throat. I make
moccasins all morning. At first my hands
kept empty, unraveled for the lives
they used to work. Now I learn to take
them back, each angry finger that demands
I mend what another will break

tomorrow. Of course, I love you;
you lean above the plastic sky,
god of our block, prince of all the foxes.
The breaking crowns are new
that Jack wore. Your third eye
moves among us and lights the separate boxes
where we sleep or cry.

What large children we are
here. All over I grow most tall
in the best ward. Your business is people,
you call at the madhouse, an oracular
eye in our nest. Out in the hall
the intercom pages you. You twist in the pull
of the foxy children who fall

like floods of life in frost.
And we are magic talking to itself,
noisy and alone. I am queen of all my sins
forgotten. Am I still lost?
Once I was beautiful. Now I am myself,
counting this row and that row of moccasins
waiting on the silent shelf.

HER KIND

I have gone out, a possessed witch,
haunting the black air, braver at night;
dreaming evil, I have done my hitch
over the plain houses, light by light:
lonely thing, twelve-fingered, out of mind.
A woman like that is not a woman, quite.
I have been her kind.

I have found the warm caves in the woods,
filled them with skillets, carvings, shelves,
closets, silks, innumerable goods;
fixed the suppers for the worms and the elves:
whining, rearranging the disaligned.
A woman like that is misunderstood.
I have been her kind.

I have ridden in your cart, driver,
waved my nude arms at villages going by,
learning the last bright routes, survivor
where your flames still bite my thigh
and my ribs crack where your wheels wind.
A woman like that is not ashamed to die.
I have been her kind.

TO A FRIEND WHOSE WORK HAS COME TO TRIUMPH

Consider Icarus, pasting those sticky wings on,
testing that strange little tug at his shoulder blade,
and think of that first flawless moment over the lawn
of the labyrinth. Think of the difference it made!
There below are the trees, as awkward as camels;
and here are the shocked starlings pumping past
and think of innocent Icarus who is doing quite well:
larger than a sail, over the fog and the blast
of the plushy ocean, he goes. Admire his wings!
Feel the fire at his neck and see how casually
he glances up and is caught, wondrously tunneling
into that hot eye. Who cares that he fell back to the sea?
See him acclaiming the sun and come plunging down
while his sensible daddy goes straight into town.

ANGEL OF CLEAN SHEETS

Angel of clean sheets do you know bed bugs?
Once in a madhouse they came like specks of cinnamon
as I lay in a chloral cave of drugs,
as old as a dog, as quiet as a skeleton.
Little bits of dried blood. One hundred marks
upon the sheet. One hundred kisses in the dark.

White sheets smelling of soap and Chlorox
have nothing to do with this night of soil,
nothing to do with barred windows and multiple locks
and all the webbing in the bed, the ultimate recoil.
I have slept in silk and in red and in black.
I have slept on sand and one fall night, a haystack.

I have known a crib. I have known the tuck-in of a child
but inside my hair waits the night I was defiled.

THOM GUNN
1929-

BLACK JACKETS

In the silence that prolongs the span
Rawly of music when the record ends,
The red-haired boy who drove a van
In weekday overalls but, like his friends,

Wore cycle boots and jacket here
To suit the Sunday hangout he was in,
Heard, as he stretched back from his beer,
Leather creak softly round his neck and chin.

Before him, on a coal-black sleeve
Remote exertion had lined, scratched, and burned
Insignia that could not revive
The heroic fall or climb where they were earned.

On the other drinkers bent together,
Concocting selves for their impervious kit,
He saw it as no more than leather
Which, taut across the shoulders grown to it,

Sent through the dimness of a bar
As sudden and anonymous hints of light
As those that shipping give, that are
Now flickers in the Bay, now lost in night.

He stretched out like a cat, and rolled
The bitterish taste of beer upon his tongue,
And listened to a joke being told:
The present was the things he stayed among.

If it was only loss he wore,
He wore it to assert, with fierce devotion,
Complicity and nothing more.
He recollected his initiation,

And one especially of the rites.
For on his shoulders they had put tattoos:
The group's name on the left, The Knights,
And on the right the slogan Born To Lose.

THE MONSTER

I left my room at last, I walked
The streets of that decaying town,
I took the turn I had renounced
Where the carved cherub crumbled down.

Eager as to a granted wish
I hurried to the cul de sac.
Forestalled by whom? Before the house
I saw an unmoved waiting back.

How had she never vainly mentioned
This lover, too, unsatisfied?
Did she dismiss one every night?
I walked up slowly to his side.

Those eyes glazed like her windowpane,
That wide mouth ugly with despair,
Those arms held tight against the haunches,
Poised, but heavily staying there:

At once I knew him, gloating over
A grief defined and realized,
And living only for its sake.
It was myself I recognized.

I could not watch her window now,
Standing before this man of mine,
The constant one I had created
Lest the pure feeling should decline.

What if I were within the house,
Happier than the fact had been

—Would he, then, still be gazing here,
The man who never can get in?

Or would I, leaving at the dawn
A suppler love than he could guess,
Find him awake on my small bed,
Demanding still some bitterness?

ADRIENNE RICH
1929-

LIVING IN SIN

She had thought the studio would keep itself;
no dust upon the furniture of love.
Half heresy, to wish the taps less vocal,
the panes relieved of grime. A plate of pears,
a piano with a Persian shawl, a cat
stalking the picturesque amusing mouse
had risen at his urging.
Not that at five each separate stair would writhe
under the milkman's tramp; that morning light
so coldly would delineate the scraps
of last night's cheese and three sepulchral bottles;
that on the kitchen shelf among the saucers
a pair of beetle-eyes would fix her own—
envoy from some black village in the mouldings . . .
Meanwhile he, with a yawn,
sounded a dozen notes upon the keyboard,
declared it out of tune, shrugged at the mirror,
rubbed at his beard, went out for cigarettes;
while she, jeered by the minor demons,
pulled back the sheets and made the bed and found
a towel to dust the table-top,
and let the coffee-pot boil over on the stove.
By evening she was back in love again,
though not so wholly, but throughout the night
she woke sometimes to feel the daylight coming
like a relentless milkman up the stairs.

PLANETARIUM

(Thinking of Caroline
Herschel, 1750–1848,
astronomer, sister of
William; and others)

A woman in the shape of a monster
a monster in the shape of a woman
the skies are full of them

a woman 'in the snow
among the Clocks and instruments
or measuring the ground with poles'

in her 98 years to discover
8 comets

she whom the moon ruled
like us
levitating into the night sky
riding the polished lenses

Galaxies of women, there
doing penance for impetuousness
ribs chilled
in those spaces of the mind

An eye,
'virile, precise and absolutely certain'
from the mad webs of Uranisborg
encountering the NOVA

every impulse of light exploding
from the core
as life flies out of us

        Tycho whispering at last
        'Let me not seem to have lived in vain'

What we see, we see
and seeing is changing

the light that shrivels a mountain
and leaves a man alive

Heartbeat of the pulsar
heart sweating through my body

The radio impulse
pouring in from Taurus

        I am bombarded yet   I stand

I have been standing all my life in the
direct path of a battery of signals
the most accurately transmitted most
untranslateable language in the universe
I am a galactic cloud so deep   so invo-
luted that a light wave could take 15
years to travel through me   And has
taken   I am an instrument in the shape
of a woman trying to translate pulsations
into images   for the relief of the body
and the reconstruction of the mind.

DEREK WALCOTT
1930-

A LETTER FROM BROOKLYN

An old lady writes me in a spidery style,
Each character trembling, and I see a veined hand
Pellucid as paper, travelling on a skein
Of such frail thoughts its thread is often broken;
Or else the filament from which a phrase is hung
Dims to my sense, but caught, it shines like steel,
As touch a line, and the whole web will feel.
She describes my father, yet I forget her face
More easily than my father's yearly dying;
Of her I remember small, buttoned boots and the place
She kept in our wooden church on those Sundays
Whenever her strength allowed;
Grey haired, thin voiced, perpetually bowed.

'I am Mable Rawlins,' she writes, 'and know both your parents';
He is dead, Miss Rawlins, but God bless your tense:
'Your father was a dutiful, honest,
Faithful and useful person.'
For such plain praise what fame is recompense?
'A horn-painter, he painted delicately on horn,
He used to sit around the table and paint pictures.'
The peace of God needs nothing to adorn
It, nor glory nor ambition.
'He is twenty-eight years buried,' she writes, 'he was called home,
And is, I am sure, doing greater work.'

The strength of one frail hand in a dim room
Somewhere in Brooklyn, patient and assured,
Restores my sacred duty to the Word.
'Home, home,' she can write, with such short time to live,

Alone as she spins the blessings of her years;
Not withered of beauty if she can bring such tears,
Nor withdrawn from the world that breaks its lovers so;
Heaven is to her the place where painters go,
All who bring beauty on frail shell or horn,
There was all made, thence their lux-mundi drawn,
Drawn, drawn, till the thread is resilient steel,
Lost though it seems in the darkening periods,
And there they return to do work that is God's.

So this old lady writes, and again I believe.
I believe it all, and for no man's death I grieve.

CORAL

This coral's shape echoes the hand
It hollowed. Its

Immediate absence is heavy. As pumice,
As your breast in my cupped palm.

Sea-cold, its nipple rasps like sand,
Its pores, like yours, shone with salt sweat.

Bodies in absence displace their weight
As your smooth body, like none other

Creates an exact absence like this stone
Set on a table with a whitening wrack

Of souvenirs. It dares my hand
To claim what lovers' hands have never known

The nature of the body of another.

TED HUGHES
1930-

HER HUSBAND

Comes home dull with coal-dust deliberately
To grime the sink and foul towels and let her
Learn with scrubbing brush and scrubbing board
The stubborn character of money.

And let her learn through what kind of dust
He has earned his thirst and the right to quench it
And what sweat he has exchanged for his money
And the blood-weight of money. He'll humble her

With new light on her obligations.
The fried, woody chips, kept warm two hours in the oven,
Are only part of her answer.
Hearing the rest, he slams them to the fire back

And is away round the house-end singing
'Come back to Sorrento' in a voice
Of resounding corrugated iron.
Her back has bunched into a hump as an insult.

For they will have their rights.
Their jurors are to be assembled
From the little crumbs of soot. Their brief
Goes straight up to heaven and nothing more is heard of it.

PIBROCH

The sea cries with its meaningless voice
Treating alike its dead and its living,
Probably bored with the appearance of heaven
After so many millions of nights without sleep,
Without purpose, without self-deception.

Stone likewise. A pebble is imprisoned
Like nothing in the Universe.
Created for black sleep. Or growing
Conscious of the sun's red spot occasionally,
Then dreaming it is the foetus of God.

Over the stone rushes the wind
Able to mingle with nothing,
Like the hearing of the blind stone itself.
Or turns, as if the stone's mind came feeling
A fantasy of directions.

Drinking the sea and eating the rock
A tree struggles to make leaves——
An old woman fallen from space
Unprepared for these conditions.
She hangs on, because her mind's gone completely.

Minute after minute, aeon after aeon,
Nothing lets up or develops.
And this is neither a bad variant nor a tryout.
This is where the staring angels go through.
This is where all the stars bow down.

SYLVIA PLATH
1932-1963

THE APPLICANT

First, are you our sort of a person?
Do you wear
A glass eye, false teeth or a crutch,
A brace or a hook,
Rubber breasts or a rubber crotch,

Stitches to show something's missing? No, no? Then
How can we give you a thing?
Stop crying.
Open your hand.
Empty? Empty. Here is a hand

To fill it and willing
To bring teacups and roll away headaches
And do whatever you tell it.
Will you marry it?
It is guaranteed

To thumb shut your eyes at the end
And dissolve of sorrow.
We make new stock from the salt.
I notice you are stark naked.
How about this suit——

Black and stiff, but not a bad fit.
Will you marry it?
It is waterproof, shatterproof, proof
Against fire and bombs through the roof.
Believe me, they'll bury you in it.

Now your head, excuse me, is empty.
I have the ticket for that.
Come here, sweetie, out of the closet.
Well, what do you think of *that?*
Naked as paper to start

But in twenty-five years she'll be silver,
In fifty, gold.
A living doll, everywhere you look.
It can sew, it can cook,
It can talk, talk, talk.

It works, there is nothing wrong with it.
You have a hole, it's a poultice.
You have an eye, it's an image.
My boy, it's your last resort.
Will you marry it, marry it, marry it.

MORNING SONG

Love set you going like a fat gold watch.
The midwife slapped your footsoles, and your bald cry
Took its place among the elements.

Our voices echo, magnifying your arrival. New statue.
In a drafty museum, your nakedness
Shadows our safety. We stand round blankly as walls.

I'm no more your mother
Then the cloud that distils a mirror to reflect its own slow
Effacement at the wind's hand.

All night your moth-breath
Flickers among the flat pink roses. I wake to listen:
A far sea moves in my ear.

One cry, and I stumble from bed, cow-heavy and floral
In my Victorian nightgown.
Your mouth opens clean as a cat's. The window square

Whitens and swallows its dull stars. And now you try
Your handful of notes;
The clear vowels rise like balloons.

DADDY

You do not do, you do not do
Any more, black shoe
In which I have lived like a foot
For thirty years, poor and white,
Barely daring to breathe or Achoo.

Daddy, I have had to kill you.
You died before I had time——
Marble-heavy, a bag full of God,
Ghastly statue with one grey toe
Big as a Frisco seal

And a head in the freakish Atlantic
Where it pours bean green over blue
In the waters off beautiful Nauset.
I used to pray to recover you.
Ach, du.

In the German tongue, in the Polish town
Scraped flat by the roller
Of wars, wars, wars.
But the name of the town is common.
My Polack friend

Says there are a dozen or two.
So I never could tell where you
Put your foot, your root,
I never could talk to you.
The tongue stuck in my jaw.

It stuck in a barb wire snare.
Ich, ich, ich, ich,

I could hardly speak.
I thought every German was you.
And the language obscene

An engine, an engine
Chuffing me off like a Jew.
A Jew to Dachau, Auschwitz, Belsen.
I began to talk like a Jew.
I think I may well be a Jew.

The snows of the Tyrol, the clear beer of Vienna
Are not very pure or true.
With my gypsy ancestress and my weird luck
And my Taroc pack and my Taroc pack
I may be a bit of a Jew.

I have always been scared of *you,*
With your Luftwaffe, your gobbledygoo.
And your neat moustache
And your Aryan eye, bright blue.
Panzer-man, panzer-man, O You——

Not God but a swastika
So black no sky could squeak through.
Every woman adores a Fascist,
The boot in the face, the brute
Brute heart of a brute like you.

You stand at the blackboard, daddy,
In the picture I have of you,
A cleft in your chin instead of your foot
But no less a devil for that, no not
Any less the black man who

Bit my pretty red heart in two.
I was ten when they buried you.
At twenty I tried to die
And get back, back, back to you.
I thought even the bones would do.

But they pulled me out of the sack,
And they stuck me together with glue.
And then I knew what to do.
I made a model of you,
A man in black with a Meinkampf look

And a love of the rack and the screw.
And I said I do, I do.
So daddy, I'm finally through.
The black telephone's off at the root,
The voices just can't worm through.

If I've killed one man, I've killed two——
The vampire who said he was you
And drank my blood for a year,
Seven years, if you want to know.
Daddy, you can lie back now.

There's a stake in your fat black heart
And the villagers never liked you.
They are dancing and stamping on you.
They always *knew* it was you.
Daddy, daddy, you bastard, I'm through.

WENDELL BERRY
1934-

MY GREAT-GRANDFATHER'S SLAVES

Deep in the back ways of my mind I see them
going in the long days
over the same fields that I have gone
long days over.

I see the sun passing and burning high
over that land from their day
until mine, their shadows
having risen and consumed them.

I see them obeying and watching
the bearded tall man whose voice
and blood are mine, whose countenance
in stone at his grave my own resembles,
whose blindness is my brand.

I see them kneel and pray to the white God
who buys their souls with Heaven.

I see them approach, quiet
in the merchandise of their flesh,
to put down their burdens
of firewood and hemp and tobacco
into the minds of my kinsmen.

I see them moving in the rooms of my history,
the day of my birth entering
the horizon emptied of their days,
their purchased lives taken back
into the dust of birthright.

I see them borne, shadow within shadow,
shroud within shroud, through all nights
from their lives to mine, long beyond
reparation or given liberty
or any straightness.

I see them go in the bonds of my blood
through all the time of their bodies.

I have seen that freedom cannot be taken
from one man and given to another,
and cannot be taken and kept.

I know that freedom can only be given,
and is the gift to the giver
from the one who receives.

I am owned by the blood of all of them
who ever were owned by my blood.
We cannot be free of each other.

DARK WITH POWER

Dark with power, we remain
the invaders of our land, leaving
deserts where forests were,
scars where there were hills.

On the mountains, on the rivers,
on the cities, on the farmlands
we lay weighted hands, our breath
potent with the death of all things.

Pray to us, farmers and villagers
of Viet Nam. Pray to us, mothers
and children of helpless countries.
Ask for nothing.

We are carried in the belly
of what we have become
toward the shambles of our triumph,
far from the quiet houses.

Fed with dying, we gaze
on our might's monuments of fire.
The world dangles from us
while we gaze.

LEROI JONES
(IMAMU AMIRI BARAKA)
1934-

LEROY

I wanted to know my mother when she sat
looking sad across the campus in the late 20's
into the future of the soul, there were black angels
straining above her head, carrying life from our ancestors,
and knowledge, and the strong nigger feeling. She sat
(in that photo in the yearbook I showed Vashti) getting
 into
new blues, from the old ones, the trips and passions
showered on her by her own. Hypnotizing me, from so far
ago, from that vantage of knowledge passed on to her
 passed on
to me and all the other black people of our time.
When I die, the consciousness I carry I will to
black people. May they pick me apart and take the
useful parts, the sweet meat of my feelings. And leave
the bitter bullshit rotten white parts
alone.

FOR HETTIE

My wife is left-handed.
Which implies a fierce determination. A complete other
worldliness. ITS WEIRD, BABY.
The way some folks
are always trying to be
different. A sin & a shame.

But then, she's been a bohemian
all of her life . . . black stockings
refusing to take orders. I sit
patiently, trying to tell her
whats right. TAKE THAT DAMM
PENCIL OUTTA THAT HAND. YOU'RE
RITING BACKWARDS. & such. But
to no avail. & it shows
in her work. Left-handed coffee,
Left-handed eggs; when she comes
in at night . . . it's her left hand
offered for me to kiss. Damm.
& now her belly droops over the seat.
They say it's a child. But
I ain't quite so sure.

DRINKING SONG

I want to die in the saddle. An enemy of civilization.
I want to walk around in the woods, fish and drink.

I'm going to be a child about it and I can't help it, I was
born this way and it makes me very happy to fish and drink.

I left when it was still dark and walked on the path to the
river, the Yellow Dog, where I spent the day fishing and drinking.

After she left me and I quit my job and wept for a year and
all my poems were born dead, I decided I would only fish and
drink.

Water will never leave earth and whisky is good for the brain.
What else am I supposed to do in these last days but fish and
drink?

In the river was a trout and I was on the bank, my heart in my
chest, clouds above, she was in NY forever and I, fishing and
drinking.

AWAKE

Limp with night fears: hellbore, wolfbane,
Marlowe is daggered, fire, volts, African vipers,
the grizzly the horses sensed, the rattlesnake
by the mailbox—how he struck at thrown rocks,
black water, framed by police, wanton wife,
I'm a bad poet broke and broken at thirty-two,
a renter, shot by mistake, airplanes and trains,
half-mast hardons, a poisoned earth, sun will
go out, car break down in a blizzard,
my animals die, fist fights, alcohol, caskets,
the hammerhead gliding under the boat near
Loggerhead Key, my soul, my heart, my brain,
my life so interminably struck with an ax
as wet wood splits bluntly, mauled into
sections for burning.

ERICA JONG
1942-

THE TEACHER

The teacher stands before the class.
She's talking of Chaucer.
But the students aren't hungry for Chaucer.
They want to devour her.
They are eating her knees, her toes, her breasts, her eyes
& spitting out
her words.
What do they want with words?
They want a real lesson!

She is naked before them.
Psalms are written on her thighs.
When she walks, sonnets divide
into octaves & sestets.
Couplets fall into place
when her fingers nervously toy
with the chalk.

But the words don't clothe her.
No amount of poetry can save her now.
There's no volume big enough to hide in.
No unabridged Webster, no OED.

The students aren't dumb.
They want a lesson.
Once they might have taken life
by the scruff of its neck
in a neat couplet.
But now
they need blood.

They have left Chaucer alone
& have eaten the teacher.

She's gone now.
Nothing remains
but a page of print.
She's past our helping.
Perhaps she's part of her students.
(Don't ask how.)

Eat this poem.

THE QUARREL

It is a rainy night
when the wind beats at your door
like a man you have turned away

He comes back trailing leaves & branches
He comes back in a shower of earth
He comes back with blades of grass
still clinging to his hair

No matter how hard he holds you
he is still elsewhere
making love to another

No matter how hard you hold him
you are still
elsewhere

Your bodies slide together
like wet grass blades
You cling & stop the raindrops
with your tongues

Later you rise
& pick the nettles from your hair
You take the leaves for clothing

Your loneliness
is a small gray hole in the rain
You rise & go knocking
at his locked front door

THE EGGPLANT EPITHALAMION

"Mostly you eat eggplant at least once a day," she explained. "A Turk won't marry a woman unless she can cook eggplant at least a hundred ways."

—*archeologist Iris Love, speaking of the cuisine on digs in Turkey.* The New York Times, *February 4, 1971*

I

There are more than a hundred Turkish poems
about eggplant.
I would like to give you all of them.
If you scoop out every seed,
you can read me backwards
like an Arabic book.
Look.

II

(Lament in Aubergine)

Oh aubergine,
egg-shaped
& as shiny as if freshly laid—
you are a melancholy fruit.
Solanum Melongena.
Every animal is sad
after eggplant.

III

(Byzantine Eggplant Fable)

Once upon a time on the coast of Turkey
there lived a woman who could cook eggplant 99 ways.
She could slice eggplant thin as paper.

She could write poems on it & batter-fry it.
She could bake eggplant & broil it.
She could even roll the seeds in banana-
flavored cigarette papers
& get her husband high on eggplant.
But he was not pleased.
He went to her father & demanded his bride-price back.
He said he'd been cheated.
He wanted back two goats, twelve chickens
& a camel as reparation.
His wife wept & wept.
Her father raved.

The next day she gave birth to an eggplant.
It was premature & green
& she had to sit on it for days
before it hatched.
"This is my hundredth eggplant recipe," she screamed.
"I hope you're satisfied!"

(Thank Allah that the eggplant was a boy).

IV

(Love & the Eggplant)

On the warm coast of Turkey, Miss Love
eats eggplant
"at least once a day."

How fitting that love should eat eggplant,
that most aphrodisiac fruit.

Fruit of the womb
of Asia Minor,

reminiscent of eggs,
of Istanbul's deep purple nights
& the Byzantine eyes of Christ.

I remember the borders of egg & dart
fencing us off from the flowers & fruit
of antiquity.
I remember the egg & tongue
probing the lost scrolls of love.
I remember the ancient faces
of Aphrodite
hidden by dust
in the labyrinth under
the British Museum
to be finally found by Miss Love
right there
near Great Russell Square.

I think of the hundreds of poems of the eggplant
& my friends who have fallen in love
over an eggplant,
who have opened the eggplant together
& swum in its seeds
who have clung in the egg of the eggplant
& have rocked to sleep
in love's dark purple boat.

II
THE
COMMENTARY

ROBERT FROST

was born in 1874 in San Francisco. Both his parents had been New England schoolteachers, but his father, a congenital nonconformer, had left Republican Massachusetts to edit a Democratic newspaper in California. After his father's death, Frost's mother took the boy, then ten years old, back to New England, where, except for two years in the English countryside, he lived the rest of his life. He chose that part of America for his special province—the titles of his books reflect his sense of local habitation and a name: *North of Boston*, *New Hampshire*, *Mountain Interval*, *West-Running Brook*, *A Further Range*, *A Witness Tree*, *In the Clearing*.

His was a crowded and hazardous growing-up. Already at eleven he tried to support himself. "I nailed shanks (drove six nails into the hollow of the sole of the shoes) in a shoe shop, and had a mouthful of nails all the summer of my twelfth year. It was piece work, and I earned better pay than I was to earn for ten years. . . . From then on I spent all my vacations either in a shoe shop or on a farm as a hired hand till I got through high school." At sixteen he pushed wagons full of metal spools in a textile mill. At eighteen he tended the dynamos and trimmed carbon lamps over the spinning machines in a Lawrence factory. A year later he taught a spring term in Salem.

He was twenty when he began as a reporter for the Lawrence *American*, twenty-one when he married his high school co-valedictorian. For the next five years he taught at his mother's private school while attending classes at Harvard. Unhappy with the curriculum, he left college after two years. His grandfather had given him a farm near Derry, New Hampshire, and ten years passed while Frost struggled with the stubborn soil in rocky pastures—"We had to blast boulders to plant potatoes."

Meanwhile, he had been writing poetry. A few poems had been printed in a magazine, but the taste of the times was for dulcet, overdecorated verse, and Frost's unvarnished, plain-speaking idiom found no favor with publishers. He had to wait until he was almost forty to see his poems printed in a book. *A Boy's Will*, composed mainly of lyrics, appeared in 1913; *North of Boston*, chiefly blank verse monologues and dialogues, followed a year later. After years of unsuccessful farming, Frost had uprooted himself and his family and had settled in the English countryside. It is a grim irony that one of the most American of American poets, unrecognized in his own country, had to have his first two books published in England. The outbreak of World War I brought him back to America and to an unexpected national response.

Suddenly famous, he became increasingly popular. Universities hurried to honor him—"I seem to be dying by degrees"—lecture halls could not accommodate all who came to hear him read poems which were reprinted in anthologies and textbooks. He was the only poet ever to receive the Pulitzer Prize four times. Each of his new books—and there were nine of them after *North of Boston*—was accorded superlative reviews. The U.S. Senate passed a congratulatory citation on his seventy-fifth birthday. Nearing eighty-seven he read one of his poems as part of the ceremonies at the inauguration of President Kennedy, sharing the platform with the President, the first time that any poet had been so honored. Toward the end of 1962 he underwent surgery for an intestinal obstruction, seemed to recover, but succumbed to an embolism. Had he lived another few weeks he would have been eighty-nine.

Whether rhymed or unrhymed, Frost's is essentially a talk-flavored poetry. A man talking to men in a Wordsworthian sense, his utterance is deceptively simple, understated, straightforward yet highly individualistic. Edward Thomas, the English poet-essayist, found the poems revolutionary in their differences; "they lack the exaggeration of rhetoric and even at first appear to lack the poetic intensity of which rhetoric is an imitation." But the intensity, and the poetry, continued to come through.

Freed from the conventional "poetic diction," Frost's poetry is revolutionary in another sense: it combines playfulness with profundity. "Mending Wall" (page 3), one of Frost's most characteristic and also one of his most popular poems, is a prime example of this combination of seriousness and raillery. Two neighboring farmers walk along opposite sides of a boundary wall to repair the winter damage. The men reveal their opposed natures in laconic phrases. One of them, the narrator, questions the need for boundaries, "Something there is that doesn't love a wall," while the other insists "Good fences make good neighbors." Some readers have found far-reaching implications in the poem. They feel it embodies one of the great problems of our time: whether national walls should be kept and strengthened for protection; or whether, since walls are barriers in the way of universal brotherhood, they should be let down. Beneath the firm presentation of two points of view, there is the teasing playfulness. Repairing the wall, the speaker says it is "just another kind of out-door game, one on a side," and that, like children, the two men use a spell to keep the boulders in place:

> Stay where you are until our backs are turned.

The badinage is continued when the speaker, suggesting that the wall is not really needed, adds whimsically:

> He is all pine and I am apple orchard.
> My apple trees will never get across
> And eat the cones under his pines, I tell him.

"Something there is that doesn't love a wall," he repeats. "That wants it down!" And his puckish spirit can't help going on:

> I could say "Elves" to him,
> But it's not elves exactly, and I'd rather
> He said it for himself.

Whimsicality mixed with wisdom is at the very heart of the poem.

"The Silken Tent" (page 5) is one of Frost's very few love poems. Subtle and alluring, it is an extended metaphor in which the loved one is compared to a silken tent, a shelter and an esthetic delight, bound "by countless silken ties of love and thought/To everything on earth." Technically, it is a curious accomplishment: a strictly rhymed Shakespearian sonnet whose fourteen lines consist of a single sentence.

"Directive" (page 6) reveals the strange, darker side of Frost. It is weighted with sadness, with a sense of loss and isolation. It carries the reader along on a slow wave of disillusioning nostalgia. Asked whether the poem is consoling or heartbreaking, Randall Jarrell replied that it is both. "Its humor and acceptance and humanity, its familiarity and elevation, give it a composed matter-of-fact magnificence. Much of the strangeness of the poem is far under the surface, or else so much on the surface, that one slides under it unnoticing. But the first wonderful sentence; the six lines about the wood's excitement; the knowledge that produces the sentence beginning 'Make yourself up a cheering song'; the plays on the word 'lost'; the whole description of the children's playhouse . . . the four wonderful conclusive sentences—these, and the whole magical and helpless mastery of the poem, are things that many have noticed and will notice. The poem is hard to understand but easy to love."

Taken as a whole, Frost's is a poetry which contemplates the world, sometimes quizzically, sometimes critically, with tolerant pity, occasional amusement, but never without love—"I had a lover's quarrel with the world." It is a poetry that is a continual rediscovery. It surprises us by making us aware of the things we always had known but had forgotten we knew. "It begins in delight and ends in wisdom."

WALLACE STEVENS

was born in 1879 in Reading, Pennsylvania. After studying at Harvard, he attended New York Law School and was admitted to the bar. He practiced law in New York for a while, but in his mid-thirties he became associated with the Hartford Accident and Indemnity Company and became one of its vice presidents, a position he held until his death at seventy-five. During the years as office worker he wrote what many consider the most imaginative poetry of the twentieth century.

Stevens resented being considered a split personality—"I prefer to think I'm just a man, not a poet part time, businessman the rest." A virtuoso of language, he relished the shine and color of words, the more exotic the better; he refused to choose between the real and the imagined world. In one of *The Letters of Wallace Stevens* he told a friend that he did not want to arrive at any irreversible conclusion. "Sometimes I believe most in the imagination for a long time and then, without reasoning about it, turn to reality and believe in that and that alone. But both of these things project themselves endlessly and I want them to do just that." "Poetry," he wrote at another time, "is my way of making the world palatable. It's the way of making one's experience, almost wholly inexplicable, acceptable." He never wrote poetry for an audience; he wrote it because "it is one of the sanctions of life." In

"The Planet on the Table," one of his last poems, he let Ariel say it for him:

> Ariel was glad he had written his poems.
> They were of a remembered time
> Or of something seen that he liked . . .
>
> It is not important that they survive.
> What mattered was that they should bear
> Some lineament or character,
>
> Some affluence, if only half-perceived,
> In the poverty of their words,
> Of the planet of which they were part.

Severely critical of his own work, Stevens' first volume, *Harmonium*, was not published until he was in his mid-forties. Much of it consisted of exquisitely modulated lines and fastidious images that live by their own logic. The sensory delight increased with his later books—a 534-page *Collected Poems*, which won the Pultizer Prize as well as a National Book Award, was followed by a 300-page *Opus Posthumous* consisting of prose writings as well as poems, opulent and verbal surprises unmatched by any of Stevens' contemporaries. In "Thirteen Ways of Looking at a Blackbird" he wrote:

> I do not know which to prefer,
> The beauty of inflections
> Or the beauty of innuendoes.

A poetry concerned with inflections and innuendoes rather than with the human condition limited Stevens' audience; even some of his admirers considered him "a poet's poet." But what Stevens achieved, he achieved with wit and gaiety and "the supreme fiction,"

> The poem of the mind in the act of finding
> What will suffice.

The four parts of "Peter Quince at the Clavier" (page 8) suggest the four parts of a small symphony. The story of Susanna and the elders, as told in the Apocrypha, is the theme with variations. The first part is a pictorial-musical statement leading into the slow movement, a languorous passage suddenly interrupted by a giddy scherzo:

> Soon, with a noise like tambourines
> Came her attendant Byzantines.

Finally sight and sound, touch and taste, bring together thought and music in a solemn coda which reconciles the body's death and beauty's deathlessness.

> Beauty is momentary in the mind—
> The fitful tracing of a portal;
> But in the flesh it is immortal.

The title of the poem is one of Stevens' amusing incongruities, for the music-making, beauty-loving Peter Quince is the carpenter-clown in *A Midsummer Night's Dream.*

In "The Poems of Our Climate" (page 11) Stevens, the esthetician, confesses that beauty, however exquisite, is not enough. "The day . . . is simplified" by the sight of a bowl of clear water holding pink and white carnations. "Still one would want more, one would need more." "There would still remain the never-resting mind"; the speechless object must be translated into human terms. "The imperfect is our paradise," the poet adds ruefully:

> Note that, in this bitterness, delight,
> Since the imperfect is so hot in us,
> Lies in flawed words and stubborn sounds.

"Of Modern Poetry" (page 12) presents, with a definiteness unusual for Stevens, the plight of the poet in a world that no longer has the support of accepted forms, subjects, standards, and beliefs, a former time when "the scene was set." Modern poetry must construct its own setting on a new stage.

> It has to be living, to learn the speech of the place.
> It has to face the men of the time and to meet
> The women of the time. It has to think about war
> And it has to find what will suffice . . . It must
> Be the finding of a satisfaction, and may
> Be of a man skating, a woman dancing, a woman
> Combing. The poem of the act of the mind.

Seldom has the case been so delicately yet so directly expressed for the need of the poet's words and the listener's responses than here, where

> . . . an invisible audience listens,
> Not to the play, but to itself, expressed
> In an emotion as of two people, as of two
> Emotions becoming one.

WILLIAM CARLOS WILLIAMS

was born in 1883 in Rutherford, New Jersey, where he lived most of his life, serving the community as a small-town family doctor and obstetrician. He was the first child of parents of mixed ancestry. His father was born in Birmingham, England, his mother in Mayaguez, Puerto Rico—"on my mother's side," wrote Williams, "there was Jewish blood via some city in Holland."

After attending the Horace Mann School in New York, Williams studied medicine in Switzerland and at the University of Pennsylvania. There were two years of internship in New York, followed by graduate work at the University of Leipzig. Then back to America as a pediatrician. Married, he became the father of two sons, one of whom eventually took over his medical practice.

Williams was in his twenty-third year when he published his first volume, a book of semi-improvised poems influenced by Pound and the Imagists. However, it was not long before he found his own outspoken, sharply flavored idiom. That his life as a general practitioner did not inhibit the work of the poet is evident from the fact that before he died at eighty he was the author of thirty-eight books of poetry, short stories, novels, essays, an autobiography, and the recipient of many awards and prizes. "As a writer," he said, "I have never felt that medicine interfered with me, but rather that it was my food and drink, the very thing which made it possible for me to write. Was I not interested in man? There the thing was right in front of me. I could touch it, feel it, smell it. It was myself, naked just as I was, without a lie, telling itself to me in its own terms."

"Unaffected," "large-hearted," "clear-sighted," "courageous," "uncompromising," are among the adjectives most often applied to Williams. He placed emphasis on the newness and vitality which resulted from contact with all that was native. Replying to those who denigrated his work as "raw" and "anti-poetic," he wrote, speaking for the younger poets, "The American writer uses a language which has been modified by time and the accidents of place to acquire a character differing greatly from that of formal English. For the appreciation of American poetry it is necessary that the reader accept this language difference from the beginning." "No ideas but in things," he exclaimed. "Emotion clusters about common things." He was always seeing the thing itself without forethought or afterthought but with great intensity of perception. In common with Whitman, Williams found nothing without use and beauty; the most tawdry things have grace "if the imagination can lighten them." He regarded the objects of his scrutiny with such affection that it has been said no one could love anything as much as Williams loved everything. Williams might have replied with aphorisms that are both simple and sensible: "The object in writing is to reveal." "The classic is the local, fully realized words marked by a place." "The end of poetry is the poem" *Paterson* synthesizes all of Williams. A book-length "personal epic," it is a most impressive and, at the same time, matter-of-fact depiction of disintegration, a complex of ugliness, factories, highways, city dumps, and all sorts of trivia, which the poet's observation and vision brings into focus.

"Tract" (page 13) is a vigorous, healthy protest, a mockery of the ostentatious and barbaric ritual of funerals. The pace of the poem is appropriately slow, a heavy walking tread, and the mourners are adjured to put aside ceremony and to

> Go with some show
> of inconvenience; sit openly—
> to the weather as to grief.
> Or do you think you can shut grief in?

"The Widow's Lament in Springtime" (page 16), written about Williams' mother, is a moving portrait that contrasts the bleak desolation of the bereaved woman and the luxuriant blooming of nature "with masses of flowers" all about her. Technically, the clipped lines are uncannily right: they are the completely realized expression of grief uttered in abrupt, short-breath sentences.

"The Yachts" (page 17) is a poem that can be read on two levels: an esthetic experience or a social document in which the expert and expensive yachts (symbol of wealth) are shown in contrast to the crude and buffeted hulls that represent labor. In her critical estimate Vivienne Koch says "The referents of the yacht-race metaphor have expanded into a moral allegory. . . . One can see it as a contest between beauty and desire, between the contradictions set up by human imperfection and the cruel, elusiveness of the 'ideal.' " In his introduction to Williams' *Selected Poems* Randall Jarrell says it is a poem "that is a paradigm of all the unjust beauty, the necessary and unnecessary injustice of the world."

"These" (page 19), a title which serves as the first line of the poem, is one of Williams' darker speculations on unhappy humanity, a recall of the desolate weeks

> when nature in its barrenness
> equals the stupidity of man.

when

> The year plunges into night
> and the heart plunges
> lower than night

> to an empty, windswept place
> without sun, stars, or moon

It is a poem of despondency, a hatred of war and a lamentation for

> the people gone that we loved,
> the beds lying empty . . .

It ends with a sad querulousness that cannot resign itself to the way of the world, a way that can live with ineffective poetry, broken music, the stopped clock.

ANNA WICKHAM

was born in 1884 in England but was taken to Australia when she was six. Her father, who had wanted to be a musician but had to earn a living as a piano-tuner, hoped that, as compensation for his failure, his daughter would be a singer. At twenty-one she returned to England, went to Paris where she studied for opera with Jean de Reszke, became his favorite pupil, and began to write poetry. She gave up her career when she married Patrick Hepburn, an astronomer who disapproved of her writing. For a while she wrote in secret, and when she triumphantly showed him some of her poems that had somehow been published, he was angered. There was a quarrel. Anna, a woman with a turbulent temper, grew furious, smashed a glass door and was certified as insane. She told David Garnett (who wrote an introduction to her *Selected Poems*) "she had taken Hall and Knight's *Algebra* with her and had spent her time in the private asylum working out quadratic equations in order to keep her mind from dwelling on her situation and to overcome her rancor." After being discharged she went back to her husband, whom in some ways she admired, and her two sons. But she was never at peace. At sixty-three she hanged herself.

In the pattern of her life, as in the patterns of her poetry, she was a precursor of Anne Sexton (page 331), who was sometimes institutionalized, and Sylvia Plath (page 341), who killed herself.

Like theirs, her poetry reveals the delight and difficulty of being a woman, and records the ambivalent struggle with complete candor. Hers is also a strange alternation, and often an amalgam, of agony and mockery, of proud defiance and painful self-denial. The character of the verse is astringent rather than charming, often harsh, twisted by its own suppressed force. She acknowledges this and says:

> Let it be something for my song
> If it is sometimes swift and strong.

There is wit here, too. She called her first book, *The Contemplative Quarry*, and her second, *The Man with the Hammer*, woman's titles with their wry implications.

"The Fired Pot" (page 21) is Anna Wickham *in petto,* but it could be almost any married woman. In its pointed simplicities we recognize the housekeeper and her routine chores—"passionate about pins, and pence, and soap"—tossed between domesticity and the repressed but recurrent dream of loveliness.

"Self-Analysis" (page 22) goes deeper. The torn self and the torturing ambivalence, cry out in every quatrain. The analysis carries not only the poet's anguish but "the incompetence of pain."

"Meditation at Kew" (page 23) is a piece of merry verse that barely conceals its serious intent. In tempo as well as in tone it is a romp, a high-spirited scherzo, a laughing appeal for "gay unions of choice."

"A Love Letter" (page 24) abandons rhyme and all attempt at lightness. Beyond sex, "completed by love," it is an expression of penetrating passion, a paradox of surrender and possession. Reserved in emphasis, it mounts from statement to sublimation until it achieves the grave and noble climax:

> I ask nothing of you, not even that you live.
> If you die, I remember you
> Till the blood in my wrists is cold.

EZRA POUND

was born in 1885 in Hailey, Idaho, but grew up in Philadelphia, where his father was Assistant Assayer of the U.S. Mint. A precocious extrovert, he entered the University of Pennsylvania at fifteen—"I knew at fifteen pretty much what I wanted to do," he recalled. "I resolved at thirty I would know more about poetry than any man living, that I would know what was accounted poetry everywhere, what part of poetry was indestructible, what part could *not* be lost in translation,* and—scarcely less important—what effects were obtainable in one language only and were utterly incapable of being translated."

After teaching at the University of Pennsylvania as "instructor with professorial functions," he taught at Wabash College and, after four months, was dismissed when a stranded actress was discovered sleeping in his bed. Pound claimed that he slept on the floor chastely wrapped in his topcoat—"all accusations were ultimately refuted save that of being 'the Latin Quarter type.' " Leaving Crawfordsville, Indiana, he landed in Venice where, at twenty-three, his first book *(A Lume Spento)* was published at his own expense. A few months later he went to London, where he es-

* Frost's definition had often been quoted: "Poetry is that which is lost in translation."

tablished himself not only as an innovator whose experiments were widely imitated, but also as a lecturer whose erudition became a legend, a literary executor of the Fenolossa collection of Chinese and Japanese poetry, a founder of the Imagist movement, a poet who persuaded Yeats to change his early mystical-lyrical manner to his later sharper, more concrete style, and who, with Eliot, was the most controversial figure in modern English poetry. In 1917 the first draft of Eliot's *The Waste Land* was published. It showed that Pound had convinced Eliot that he should curtail the poem; Eliot acknowledged the advice by reshaping the poem and dedicating it to Pound as *il miglior fabbro,* "the better craftsman."

From London Pound went to Paris, composed music, an opera about François Villon, discovered the vorticist sculptor, Gaudier-Brzeska and Douglas' Social Credit movement, which led to Pound's preoccupation with "false credit" and usury—"usury, that's at the heart of all corruption, that's what's eating humanity alive."

Repudiating America as completely corrupt, Pound went to Italy, settled in the seacoast town of Rapallo and, at the outbreak of World War II, began broadcasting propaganda from Rome. He glorified Mussolini, excoriated Roosevelt, and attacked the United States for being controlled by "kikes." When the U.S. Army invaded Italy, he was arrested and indicted for treason. After an internment near Pisa, where, at sixty, he composed the *Pisan Cantos,* he was brought to Washington but evaded trial when psychiatrists certified he was of unsound mind. After twelve years' confinement in St. Elizabeth's Hospital, he was released. At seventy-three, broken in health and spirit, he returned to Italy, where he was cared for by his mistress, the retired violinist, Olga Rudge. (He had been married to the former Dorothy Shakespear, who was known as "Pound's official widow.") A guarded recluse in his eighties, he saw few people and spoke little to anyone. He died at eighty-seven in Venice.

Pound's shorter poems, most of them acrid in tone, ironic in mood, and colloquial in style, have been generally praised for their spare but incisive eloquence. On the other hand, the *Cantos*

—one hundred and nine had been published by Pound's mid-seventies—have stirred endless interpretations and have occasioned diametrically opposed estimates. Critics were divided between those who considered the work (a mingling of subjects and counter-subjects, history and mythology, fragments of classic literature and contemporary events) an almost incomprehensible ramble of unconnected jottings and fractured private associations, and those who considered it a colossal creation, a masterpiece of extraordinary soliloquies. Here, for example, are the first eight lines of Canto II:

> Hang it all, Robert Browning,
> there can be but the one "Sordello."
> But Sordello, and my Sordello?
> Lo Sordels si fo di Mantovana.
> So-shu churned in the sea.
> Seal sports in the spray-whited circles of cliff-wash,
> Sleek head, daughter of Lir, eyes of Picasso
> Under black fur-hood, lithe daughter of Ocean . . .

There was, however, no question about Pound's influence. More than 150 critical analyses of his work have appeared in print. He was a pioneer who fought against complacency of thought and expression. He stressed the power of the creative word—"make it new"—in contradistinction to the commonly accepted outworn poetic idioms. "Above all," said Louis Simpson, speaking for the younger poets, "he gave us a language to write in."

"Portrait d'une Femme" (page 25) is a prolonged metaphor which draws a detailed picture of a London hostess whose mind is like the Sargasso Sea, a section of the Atlantic clogged with seaweed, wreckage, and all sorts of buried treasure—

> Ideas, old gossip, oddments of all things,
> Strange spars of knowledge and dimmed wares of price.

She, too, has collected treasures from many sources ("Great minds have sought you—lacking someone else") and, though she says and does nothing that is original ("nothing that's quite your own"), she is

> a person of some interest, one comes to you
> And takes strange gain away.

Besides presenting the image of the woman, the poet takes pleasure in the added counter-play of words. The reader, too, will relish the double meanings of "interest," "gain," and "pay."

"The Rest" (page 26) is a protest against everything that Pound detested and a defense of helpless minorities: artists scorned by small-town prejudice, nonconformers thwarted by "the system," all those dispossessed and enslaved. It is, moreover, an appeal to those "persisting to successes" to speak up against ignorance and hatred. Pound offers his own career as an example:

> Take thought:
> I have weathered the storm,
> I have beaten out my exile.

The title of "The Lake Isle" (page 27) is a take-off on Yeats' famous lyric, "The Lake Isle of Innisfree." Like Yeats' poem, Pound's also expresses a yearning for happiness. However, instead of longing for a small cabin "of clay and wattles made," Pound appeals to the gods for a litte tobacco shop—or, he adds slyly, any profession where one is not continually troubled with the need to use one's brains.

MARIANNE MOORE

was born in 1887 in St. Louis, Missouri. After graduating from Bryn Mawr she taught stenography at the United States Indian School at Carlisle, Pennsylvania, and for a while was an assistant at a branch of the New York Public Library. In 1925 she was appointed editor of *The Dial*, the most prestigious literary magazine of the period, and held that position until its demise in 1929.

Although she had written a considerable amount of poetry, she was too modest to submit it for publication; it was not until she was in her mid-thirties that friends had her first volume published without her knowledge. Six books and twenty years later, her *Collected Poems* received all the most esteemed poetry honors for 1951: the Pulitzer Prize, the Bollingen Prize, and the National Book Award. It was followed by three more volumes of her "small ingenuities," by which time she had been acclaimed by critics and creators as one who had widened the field of modern poetry. T. S. Eliot said that hers was "part of the durable poetry written in our time," and William Carlos Williams declared: "There is no better poet writing in America today or one who touches so deftly a great range of our thought." Alluding to her rhyming of accented with unaccented syllables, W. H. Auden declared: "The endless musical and structural possibilities of Miss Moore's invention are a treasure which future English poets will be able to plunder. I have already stolen a great deal myself."

Miss Moore was exceptionally modest about her accomplishment. "Poetry," she said, "is a peerless proficiency of the imagination. I prize it, but am myself an observer; I can see no reason for calling my work poetry except that there is no other category in which to put it." Asked why, besides writing about "imaginary gardens with real toads in them" (an image she took from Yeats), she chose such subjects as baseball, racing, and the preservation of historic buildings, she replied: "Subjects choose me . . . I never know just how a poem will develop or end. I lie in wait like a leopard on a branch-strained metaphor." Although many modern poets discarded rhyme, she was one who believed that rhyme would persist because of its surprising ingenuousness. "With me it began with Mother Goose, and I have never tired of Gilbert and Sullivan."

Hers was a unique method of composition. She made poems like mosaics, interspersing quotations with keen descriptions. Technically it is a peculiarly measured verse-making in which, instead of using stress meters, the syllables seem to be strictly counted. This makes for a pleasurable combination of tension and looseness; the rhymes often occur on the weak syllables and, tugging and resisting, the poem soars like a kite. "With no resistance," she said, "a kite staggers and falls; whereas if it catches the right current of air it can rise, darting and soaring as it pulls and fights the wind." Likening the poet to the scientist, she said that both are "willing to waste effort. To be hard on himself is one of the main struggles of each. Each is attentive to clues, each must narrow the choice, must strive for precision."

It was precision and clarity for which she continually strove. Objecting to what she felt was planned obscurity on the part of certain poets, she wrote:

> . . . complexity is not a crime
> but carry it to the point of murkiness
> and nothing is plain . . .

The opaque allusion, the simulated
flight upward, accomplishes nothing.

A most discriminating craftsman, she valued instinct as much as intelligence. "There is," she wrote in "Critics and Connoisseurs," "a great amount of poetry in unconscious fastidiousness." She died, after a long illness, in her eighty-fifth year.

"Nevertheless" (page 28) and "The Mind is an Enchanting Thing" (page 30) synthesize Marianne Moore's individualistic qualities, her probing curiosity and microscopic scrutiny, her fine sensibility, and her technique: the truncated lines and half-hidden rhymes.

"Nevertheless" begins playfully

you've seen a strawberry
that's had a struggle; yet
was, where the fragments met,

a hedgehog or a star-
fish for the multitude
of seeds.

and ends with a terse philosophic cadence:

What is there

like fortitude! What sap
went through that little thread
to make the cherry red!

"The Mind is an Enchanting Thing" is built on a series of disparate yet consistent similes and metaphors: "like the glaze on a katydid-wing," "like Gieseking playing Scarlatti," "like the apteryx-awl" (the long slender bill of the nearly extinct tailless New

Zealand bird), "the kiwi's rain-shawl of haired feathers"—all properties of the mind which

> has memory's ear
>   that can hear without
> having to hear.

"The Wood-Weasel" (page 32) is a brilliant adaptation of an old device. It is not only a sympathetic picture of the much-scorned polecat or skunk, in which (adopting a euphemism) the poet champions the little creature and lifts it from its disreputable associations, but is also a rhymed acrostic in reverse. Unlike most acrostics, in which the first letters of each line when read downwards spell out a name, the first letters of the lines in "The Wood-Weasel" must be read from the bottom line to the top of the first verse, and then from the bottom line to the top of the second verse, thereby revealing the name of the person to whom the poem is dedicated—a neat and amusing trick of poetic legerdemain.

T. S. ELIOT

was born in 1888 in St. Louis, Missouri. Youngest of six children whose ancestors were Puritan New Englanders—his Boston grandfather founded the first Unitarian church in St. Louis—he was educated at Milton Academy, Harvard, the Sorbonne, and Merton College, Oxford. In his mid-twenties he settled in England and became a schoolmaster. After four years he discovered he disliked teaching and took a job as a bank clerk. Married at twenty-seven, a few years later he obtained a position with a London publishing house, rose to full partnership, edited a quarterly, *The Criterion*, and, in his fortieth year, became a naturalized British subject. To those who questioned the move he explained: "Here I am making a living, enjoying my friends here. I don't like being a squatter; I might as well take the full responsibility." He added that he was now "Anglo-Catholic in religion, royalist in politics, and classicist in literature."

Eliot's youthful poems composed while he was in his late teens were written in the romantic style of the period. While he was at Harvard he discovered the French symbolists, and his approximations of their manner were printed in the *Harvard Advocate.* His first volume, *Prufrock and Other Observations*, appeared when Eliot was twenty-nine. The poems voiced the arid culture and creeping disillusion of the time; they echoed one of Eliot's favorite quotations from Dryden's "Secular Masque":

All, all of a piece throughout
  Thy chase had a beast in view;
Thy wars brought nothing about;
  Thy lovers were all untrue.
'Tis well an age is out,
  And time to begin a new.

The expression of disillusion was enlarged and intensified in *The Waste Land.* Eliot defended himself against the charge that he was preoccupied with what is ugly and repulsive instead of being comforted by the pleasurable elements of existence. "The essential advantage for a poet," he wrote in *The Use of Poetry*, "is not to have a beautiful world with which to deal; it is to be able to see beneath both beauty and ugliness; to see the boredom, and the horror, and the glory."

The Waste Land, a five-part poem of some 450 lines, was published when Eliot was thirty-four. It came as a shock that was a revelation of Eliot and something of a revolution in poetry. William Carlos Williams said that it "wiped out our world as if an atom bomb had been dropped on it"; Pound, who had edited the first draft and considered himself the poem's midwife, declared it was "enough to make the rest of us shut up shop." Eliot himself modestly disclaimed any grandiose intention. In a statement which his second wife, Valerie Eliot, placed as a conspicuous epigraph to the transcript of the original draft published in 1971, Eliot had written: "Various critics have done me the honor to interpret the poem in terms of criticism of the contemporary world, have considered it, indeed, as an important piece of social criticism. To me it was only the relief of a personal and wholly insignificant grouse against life."

Most of *The Waste Land* was composed while Eliot was recovering from a nervous breakdown in a clinic in Lausanne, Switzerland. His first marriage was a desperately unhappy one, due to

Vivien Eliot's frequent mental collapses, and *The Waste Land* was largely a reflection of the disasters which can overtake love. It is a poem of compulsion, in which (in spite of Eliot's disclaimers) there is expressed a disgust of the modern world, an exposure of the drouth and detritus of civilization, and a repulsive attitude toward sex. But it is also a magnificent mixture of "memory and desire," justifying Eliot's exploration of "the boredom, and the horror, and the glory."

Eliot's later work marked a divergence in widely different directions. There were the deeply religious *Four Quartets*, which to Eliot represented "the intolerable wrestle with words and meaning," and which many believe to be a philosophic triumph uniting sense and spirit. There were the plays, also widely different: the solemn and disturbing dramas, such as *The Rock* and *Murder in the Cathedral*, emphasizing "the intersection of the timeless with time"; *The Cocktail Party* and *The Confidential Clerk*, provocative and sometimes painful comedies. And there was the surprise of *Old Possum's Book of Practical Cats*, a book of nimble light verse extolling the vast variety of felines.

At sixty Eliot was awarded the Nobel Prize for "work as a trail-blazing pioneer of modern poetry." In the same year he was honored by King George VI with the distinguished Order of Merit. His seventieth birthday brought out salvos of praise and a dozen volumes analyzing his impact; one bibliography listed almost 300 critical studies. He was seventy-six when he died in his London home.

The theme of "The Hollow Men" (page 33) is a distillation of the disillusion and despair of *The Waste Land*. The atmosphere of desolation and hopelessness is suggested by the cryptic epigraphs: "Mistah Kurtz—he dead" and "A penny for the Old Guy." It was Kurtz in Joseph Conrad's *Heart of Darkness* who went down to death "condemning, loathing all the universe," and November 5th is remembered in England as the day when girls and boys dress up in mockery of the conspiring Guy Fawkes, begging for pennies, until his effigy is burned "with a bang" in a bonfire. Eliot rivets our attention upon an exhausted, meaningless world:

"shape without form, shade without colour,/ Paralysed force, gesture without motion." Figures stuffed with straw, lifeless Guy Fawkes-like effigies, gather in a lonely valley of dying stars. In this deadliness, "death's twilight kingdom," nothing can expect a response; even the words of St. Matthew ("For Thine is the Kingdom") are uncompleted, broken off "between the desire and the spasm." Death comes without dignity; man approaches his shabby end by way of a distorted nursery rhyme—"Here we go round the mulberry bush" turns into "Here we go round the prickly pear"—and a child's game becomes a tormented litany of frustration as the world ends

Not with a bang but a whimper.

"The Rock" (page 37) is a kind of cantata which gradually moves toward affirmation, to the Visible Church and the Light Invisible. But it is overcast with the apathy and cynicism of the contemporary world.

I journeyed to London, to the timekept City;
Where the river flows, with foreign flotations.
There I was told: we have too many churches
And too few chop-houses.

The beginning of the third section is especially bitter. The voice of the Lord is heard in a quiet but trenchant excoriation of a "wretched generation of enlightened men/ Betrayed in the mazes of your ingenuities." Appraising man's future, Eliot, by way of the Lord, wryly observes:

And the wind shall say: "Here were decent godless people:
Their only monument the asphalt road
And a thousand lost golf balls."

"Journey of the Magi" (page 39) is Eliot's troubled meditation on the death of the old and the birth of the new. Surprisingly yet appropriately, Eliot opens the poem with a quotation from one of Lancelot Andrewes' seventeenth century sermons. Nothing is said about the star that guided the Magi. The one who narrates the story in a matter-of-fact way remembers the bad weather and the annoying details of the journey: the ailing camels, the attendants complaining

> And running away, and wanting their liquor and women,
> And the night-fires going out, and the lack of shelters,
> And the cities hostile and the towns unfriendly,
> And the villages dirty and charging high prices:

The narrator wonders whether it was worth the hard time, especially when he remembers the summer palaces the Magi had left, the sunny terraces, "And the silken girls bringing sherbet." But he also remembers a blind drive, an unconscious faith, that urged them on. The arrival in the temperate valley is enriched with details that are not only significant but dramatically symbolic. The "three trees on the low sky" inevitably connote the three wooden crosses on Golgotha; the "six hands at an open door dicing for pieces of silver" suggest the pieces of silver delivered to Judas.

The end is curiously ambiguous; it culminates in a query. The narrator, one of the legendary Wise Men, cannot be sure that he has experienced the death of an old belief and the miraculous birth of a new dispensation. Nevertheless, he would endure the hardships and the agony again, knowing he can no longer worship the old gods.

was born in 1889 in Savannah, Georgia. When he was ten years old his father shot the boy's mother and killed himself—a trauma which some believe may account for the melancholy and the sense of desolation which pervades much of Aiken's work. After the tragedy, the boy was brought up by relatives in New England. He entered Harvard, married a Canadian, by whom he had three children—John, Jane, and Joan, all of them gifted writers—lived for a while in England, then spent most of his life alternating between Massachusetts and Georgia. A faintly disguised autobiography, *Ushant*, is not only an account of his varied backgrounds, his marriages, and changing associations, but is also a brilliant reconstruction of a troubled creative spirit.

One of the most prolific and versatile of American poets, at the age of eighty Aiken had published thirty volumes of poetry—his *Collected Poems* ran to more than a thousand pages—five remarkable novels, five collections of striking short stories, two books of criticism, three books for children, a couple of anthologies, and a "seizure of limericks," as well as the autobiographical *Ushant*.

Recipient of all sorts of citations and awards, including the Pulitzer Prize, the Bollingen Prize, and the prestigious Gold Medal from the National Institute of Arts and Letters, Aiken nevertheless never won the large audience he deserved. He received, as the London *Times Literary Supplement* noted, "a recognition too grudging for it to be satisfactory to those who value his writing for its intrinsic worth: for its 'world of symbols shimmering with ambivalences and ambiguities,' and for the fact that it is, unlike much verse of our time, always the spoken word." The article suggested that the poet's penchant for wrapping his themes in "tissue upon tissue of proviso and aspect" may be a reason for Aiken's inability to win unreserved acclaim.

There were other reasons for Aiken's lack of popular appeal —he had been called "the best-known unread poet of the twentieth century." Ignoring trends of the moment, he was never in fashion, never prominent in the press. In an era of publicity-seekers he declined to attend literary gatherings or read his poetry as a platform performance. His position was never "finalized"; critics differed widely concerning his place in contemporary literature.

That place has never been determined. Some contend that Aiken is primarily and preeminently a lyric poet, while others maintain that his later and longer philosophical-metaphysical soliloquies are his most important achievements. The most valuable of his poems, according to Benjamin DeMott, "testify unequivocally to the dependence of comprehensive human knowledge on meditated experience, self-siftings that purify irony of mockery and cross-light despair with attachment." Although there is little likelihood of agreement concerning a final estimate, there is no question about the range and richness of Aiken's productivity.

"A Letter from the Grass" (page 41) and "Waking in the Morning" are semi-companion poems, subtle and tender and curiously attached. The first holds the reader with statements that are alternately forthright and ambiguously veiled, moving with the mysterious

Something of the noiseless unfolding of the shutters of daybreak
in the great silence of morning, something too
of the manifold infoldings of nightfall . . .

The second carries the awareness of life's mutability further. The sleeper awakes with half-drowsy visual perceptions and half-aroused mental speculations:

> the light moves a trace to the right, and the heartbeat
> shifts as in sympathy too with the light
> the ear is now tuned to a new pitch of light . . .
>
> our shadow precedes us and gives us our shape
> and only in this shall we find out our dancing
> and only in dancing find out our escape.

"The Census-Takers" (page 43) is more direct, a series of random, seemingly inconsequential yet significant and even ominous questions. They are questions that challenge; they will "take you to task" while

> The truth will be hurrying home, and it's time you knew.

ARCHIBALD MACLEISH

son of a Scottish merchant and a clergyman's daughter, was born in 1892 in Glencoe, Illinois. He was graduated from Yale University and Harvard Law School, served in the Field Artillery during World War I, became an attorney in Boston, but within three years gave up the practice of law for literature. For a while he was one of the editors of *Fortune* magazine, after which he was appointed Librarian at the Library of Congress. On the outbreak of World War II he became Director of the Office of Facts and Figures, one of President Roosevelt's close advisors, and Assistant Secretary of State. At fifty-seven he held the position of Boylston Professor of Oratory and Rhetoric at Harvard.

MacLeish's detractors say that it is oratory and rhetoric which characterize MacLeish's poetry. But the critical majority differs from so sweeping a disposal. MacLeish won the Pulitzer Prize three times: for *Conquistador*, a saga-poem in loose terza rima; for *Collected Poems*, which also received the Bollingen Prize and the National Book Award; and for the verse play, *J.B.*

By the time MacLeish had reached his mid-sixties he was the author of nineteen volumes of poetry, several collections of essays and articles, plays for radio, and the successful dramatization of the Book of Job, *J.B.* which, in a theatrical-theological debate, presented the paradox of man's indebtedness to a god who is in debt to man.

A poet who was also a public figure, MacLeish had to suffer slings and arrows because of his outrageous good fortune. Although he was accused of writing to suit the fluctuations of taste and assuming the role of oracular prophet, even MacLeish's most disparaging critics acknowledged his extraordinary craftsmanship. He enlarged the gamut of sound effects with concealed and consonantal rhymes. His, moreover, was a persuasive tone, clear, energetic, and often noble. Much of it had what MacLeish listened for in a poem: "the clean, sharp stroke which is heard when the axe goes into the living wood."

"You, Andrew Marvell" (page 44) is a poem built on symbols and suspense. Quietly increasing in tension, the suspense is heightened by a depiction of the gradual approach of night; it is intensified by the unpunctuated progress; it is sustained by the gathering force of the long single sentence. Twilight creeps inevitably on with "the always rising of the night." The words themselves furnish vivid contrasts. The pale, almost colorless light and the unearthly chill are set off by warm and exotically colored syllables: *Ecbatan, Persia, Baghdad, Arabia, Palmyra, Crete,* and *Kermanshah,* names that suggest a strange enchantment. The title is a flashback to Marvell's poem "To His Coy Mistress." In it Marvell declared he would be willing to wait for the consummation of his love were it not that the sun refuses to stand still,

> . . . and at my back I always hear
> Time's winged chariot hurrying near.

And here, "face downward in the sun," the twentieth-century MacLeish shares the fear and foreboding of the dark, "the deserts of vast eternity," that troubled the seventeenth century Marvell.

"The End of the World" (page 46) is a peculiar poem: a strict sonnet that is calmly terrifying. Its setting is also peculiar: a circus tent; and, as in "You, Andrew Marvell," the apprehension of what is to come is heightened by the suspended single sentence while the canvas top blows off. There, while the performers, the freaks, and the animals are going through their usual routines,

> There with vast wings across the canceled skies,
> There in the sudden blackness, the black pall
> Of nothing, nothing, nothing—nothing at all.

"Not Marble Nor the Gilded Monuments" (page 47) is a title taken from Shakespeare's fifty-fifth sonnet which begins:

> Not marble nor the gilded monuments
> Of princes shall outlive this powerful rhyme,
> But you shall shine more bright in these contents
> Than unswept stone besmeared with sluttish time.

and ends:

> So, till the judgment that yourself arise
> You live in this, and dwell in lovers' eyes.

Offering a tribute to the beloved one, MacLeish echoes Shakespeare's adoration. However, modestly, he hesitates to assure her of immortality or claim that she "shall outlive this powerful rhyme." Yet, in his very understatements, MacLeish creates one of the most eloquent and moving love poems.

E. E. CUMMINGS

was born in 1894 in Cambridge, Massachusetts. His father, who became minister of The South Congregational Church in Boston, taught at Harvard, and it was from Harvard that Cummings received his master's degree. During World War I he served with an ambulance corps and, because of a stupidity on the part of a French official, was detained for three months in a French concentration camp. This experience was recorded in *The Enormous Room*, a classic among war books.

An unusually versatile creator, Cummings wrote plays; a ballet based on *Uncle Tom's Cabin*; a journal of his trip to Russia; *six nonlectures,* originally delivered as the Charles Eliot Norton Lectures at Harvard; as well as *A Miscellany* containing social, political, and cultural critiques. There was also a portfolio of his pictures entitled "CIOPW," indicating that the collection included work done in Charcoal, Ink, Oil, Pencil, and Watercolor. But it was the spontaneous individuality of his poetry which established Cummings as one of the twentieth century's most original poets.

One phase of Cummings' originality was his predilection for lower case letters and typographical oddities, lyrics fragmented without punctuation or interrupted with punctuation where the reader least expected it. Cummings emphasized the significance of his words by separating them or their syllables so they would stand out sharply on the printed pages and compel the reader's attention.

As poetry, Cummings' is both lovely and limited. At its worst the poetry is sentimental, full of trite adjectives, and a reliance on the stock properties of popular verse: life, death, spring, roses, and rhetoric. "Many poems," wrote a critic in the London *Times Literary Supplement*, "sound as if they were written to provide a lively setting for one phrase, a gem the poet was reluctant to leave aside." At its best the poetry is vigorous, delicate, and delightful—"nobody, not even the rain, has such small hands," "wholly to be a fool while spring is in the world my blood approves"—a poetry where feeling is first and also last, a poetry which often justifies Marianne Moore's summary of Cummings' quality as "indivisible, undismemberable joy."

Cummings' first complete collection, *Poems: 1923–1954*, a book of 468 pages, displayed the range of his accomplishment, from the early prettified archaisms to the later more satiric and sombre realities. It received the National Book Award. It was followed by another collection of ninety-five poems and a posthumous *73 Poems*. Cummings died after suffering a stroke in 1962.

"my father moved through dooms of love" (page 49) is characteristic of Cummings in several ways. The idiom is singular: ordinary syntax is mixed with strange constructions like "through sames of am through haves of give." Except for three capitals, lower case letters are used throughout the seventeen quatrains. Conventional rhymes alternate with half-rhymes and assonances such as "love" and "give," "which" and "touch," "beyond" and "stand." But what makes the poem distinguished is its integral emotion. What threatens to become sentimental turns into honest sentiment, with images as noble as "his shoulders marched against the dark" and similes as homely as "his sorrow was as true as bread." More direct than Cummings' virtuoso performances, it ends with an almost stark simplicity:

> because my father lived his soul
> love is the whole and more than all.

It is interesting to compare Cummings' tribute to his father with Dylan Thomas' "Do Not Go Gentle into that Good Night" on page 105.

"now that, more nearest even than your fate" (page 52) is an announcement of another kind of love, amatory rather than filial. Love is a word that runs like a Wagnerian leitmotif through all Cummings' work—"you being in love/will tell who softly asks in love" . . . "love is the every only god/who spoke this earth so glad and big" . . . "love is a spring at which/crazy they drink" . . . "lovers are those whose lips/smash unimagined sky." So here, after summoning "this miracle of summer night" with "her trillion secrets touchably alive" and "all mysteries which i or you . . . could only fancy we should never know," Cummings does not hesitate to end with a lover's grandiose hyperbole:

> that hugest whole creation may be less
> incalculable than a single kiss.

Although the odd typography and peculiar spacing tend to conceal the classic form, the poem is a sonnet.

HART CRANE

life was a tragedy of physical restlessness and psychical rootlessness. It began in Garretsville, Ohio, in 1899 and ended a little less than thirty-three years later in the Gulf of Mexico. His was a miserable upbringing. There were endless quarrels between his father, a good-natured business man, and his neurotic, sex-loathing, self-pitying mother. Crane never finished high school; his sporadic attempts to earn a living were always unsuccessful. He worked in a printshop, became a riveter in a shipyard, sold candy in one of his father's stores, and was a cub reporter for a few weeks. He loathed all these occupations.

Crane began writing poetry in his early teens and had his first serious homosexual affair before he was twenty—"I have never had devotion returned before like this, nor ever found a soul, mind, and body so worthy of devotion. Probably I never shall again."

In his twenty-first year Crane made his debut as a professional poet when *The Dial* published and paid him ten dollars for "My Grandmother's Love Letters." "What I want to get," Crane wrote, "is an 'interior' form, a form that is so thorough and intense as to dye the words themselves with a peculiarity of meaning, slightly different from the ordinary definitions of them." He hoped to accomplish this by stretching suggestibility to its limits, by a purposeful derangement of the senses (often achieved by excessive drinking), and by using a concatenation of images which he called a "logic of metaphor" that surpassed "our so-called pure logic." Poetry for him was a brilliant union of incongruities. In "For the Marriage of Faustus and Helen," for example, Helen is placed in the setting of a street car with "the Dionysian revels of her court transferred to a metropolitan roof garden with a jazz orchestra and the *katharsis* of the fall of Troy approximated in the World War."

At twenty-three Crane began work on his most ambitious project, *The Bridge*, a flawed but powerful semi-epic composed of headlong images and haunting hallucinatory phrases, a work which Crane thought of as "the mystical synthesis of America." At twenty-seven he published his first book, *White Buildings*. Even those who found it bizarre could not ignore such flashes of vision as "Where the cedar leaf divides the sky," "in sapphire arenas of the hills," "permit me voyage, love, into your hands," and his picture of the sea as "this great wink of eternity."

Crane's life was a series of unhappy confrontations, rages, drunken brawls, getting himself beaten up in waterfront bars, being arrested in New York, Paris, Marseilles. A Guggenheim Fellowship gave him an excuse to go to Mexico where he became more disorderly than ever. He was no longer capable of feeling anything except under violent and brutal shock. In his thirty-third year he boarded a ship to take him back to the United States, but while the ship was still in the Gulf of Mexico, he jumped overboard. The body was never recovered.

Estimates of Crane's accomplishment differ widely. Robert Lowell called him "the Shelley of our age," and W. R. B. Lewis ranked him as "one of the finest modern poets in our language and one of the dozen major poets in American history." Other appraisals were more critical. F. R. Leavis found Crane's *The Bridge* "a wordy chaos," and Denis Donoghue held that Crane "cultivated intensity at the expense of every other poetic value . . . He was a poet whose reach far exceeded his grasp; greater in short poems than in long poems; greater in stanza than in poem;

greater in line than in stanza. Perhaps it is significant that his poems stay in the mind as phrases, often drawing away from their setting."

"Voyages" and "The Broken Tower" are among the shorter poems in which individual phrases remain in the mind if only because of their rhetorical grandeur.

"Voyages: II" (page 53) is composed of a series of seemingly unrelated images. The images are not presented in a narrative sequence but occur simultaneously, side by side, and follow Crane's concept of a "logic of metaphor." His theory of "interior form" is upheld if not proved by the accumulating visionary figures of speech—"this great wink of eternity," "scrolls of silver snowy sentences," "the crocus lustres of the stars," "adagios of islands," "the seal's wide spindrift gaze toward paradise"—visions held in five stanzas of five lines each, a virtuoso performance of design and suggestion.

"The Broken Tower" (page 54) is among Crane's most controlled and strictly rhymed poems, a control which Crane was able to form out of his chaos. It is also one of his most impassioned poems. It communicates what Crane recognized as "an absolute music in the air." Influenced by Eliot, as was much of Crane's poetry, it is also a repudiation of Eliot's pessimism and world weariness. "I would apply as much of Eliot's erudition and technique as I can absorb," Crane wrote, "and assemble toward a more positive or ecstatic goal." In spite of his dismal life Crane never lost his essentially ecstatic dream, a dream of love which found incomplete expression in his "Voyages" and which, "healed, original now, and pure," concludes "The Broken Tower":

> . . . visible wings of silence sown
> In azure circles, widening as they dip
>
> The matrix of the heart, lift down the eye
> That shrines the quiet lake and swells a tower . . .
> The commodious, tall decorum of that sky
> Unseals her earth, and lifts love in its shower.

LANGSTON HUGHES

was born in 1902 in Joplin, Missouri, was class poet in his high school, and at eighteen taught English in Mexico. He worked his way through Spain and Italy and was a busboy in Washington where he was discovered by the poet Vachel Lindsay who read several of his poems to an audience in the very hotel in which Hughes carried dishes. His first poem printed in a nationally known magazine was "The Negro Speaks of Rivers," and the title poem of his first book, *The Weary Blues* was awarded a prize by *Opportunity*, a pioneering periodical that fostered creative work by blacks.

Hughes' subsequent works—eight volumes of poetry, four of fiction, six for young people, and three of humor—were instrumental in emphasizing the revival of Negro art. Hughes was one of the first to project the spirit of the blues in poetry and to establish its principles. Hospitalized at sixty-five, he died May 22, 1967.

"Young Gal's Blues" (page 56) is typical of the melancholy strain of the blues which express in almost childlike verse the troubles and trials of an aggrieved race. The blues have a strict poetic pattern: the first and second lines are repeated with only slight variations. "The mood of the blues is almost always despondency," wrote Hughes, "but when they are sung, people usually laugh." "Young Gal's Blues" is a perfect example of the form.

"Madam and the Rent Man" (page 57) has the tone of the blues, but its form is tighter and its application is particularized. It is a metropolitan poem, a poem of the crowded city with its dirty ghetto, its broken down apartments, its exploited inhabitants. Harsh it is, and Hughes accentuates its ugliness with grim humor.

was born in 1904 in Austin, Minnesota. His education ranged from Dartmouth College to St. John's (University of Cambridge) and the Harvard Graduate School. He taught English at St. Mark's School and tutored the son of the King of Siam. Before his first university appointment, he worked in a department store as well as in a slaughterhouse, served as an aerial gunnery instructor in World War II and, after his discharge, combined the functions of poet, teacher, and lecturer with that of manager of his wife's family business which manufactured floor polishes. Between writing poems he wrote *Helpful Hints to Homemakers*, a pamphlet in praise of Butcher's Wax.

Eberhart's first volume, *A Bravery of Earth*, published in his twenty-sixth year, revealed an almost physical exuberance. The sense of what Robert Lowell called his "stately jagged innocence" characterizes his subsequent works. Eberhart's is a paradoxical idiom; it is plain, often prosaic, but it works its way up to a contemplation that attains moments of sheer rhapsody. His books—by his late sixties there were ten of them—had won such coveted awards as the Pulitzer and Bollingen prizes and a Consultantship in Poetry at the Library of Congress.

Eberhart's position as a poet has been variously appraised. Even those who assert that he overindulges his gift and harms himself with his own prolixity grant that, despite his many failures, his successes are brilliant. Attention has repeatedly been called to the arresting imagination of such opening lines as "If I could only live at the pitch that is near madness," "My death was arranged by special plans in Heaven," "In prisons of established craze," "My bones flew apart. They flew to the sky," "In a hard intellectual light," "Now is the air made of chiming balls," "My golden and my fierce assays, / My bold and sudden thunderbolts," "The grave's seed will get some monstrous bloom."

"The Groundhog" (page 59) is one of Eberhart's most quoted poems. The poet's insight depicts the decay of a living thing, a "senseless change" and relates it to the mystical emotions roused by life into death and dissolution, an ordinary tragedy occurring throughout time, emotions that have stirred conquerors like Alexander, philosophers like Montaigne, and ecstatic nuns like Saint Theresa.

"If I Could Only Live at the Pitch that is Near Madness" (page 61) is an excellent illustration of Eberhart's casual but searching self-examination. The longing to experience everything as it is in childhood, "violent, vivid, and of infinite possibility," is pitted against the actual world with its "realm of complexity," "where nothing is possible but necessity."

"Man and Nature" (page 62) combines clear vision and speculative imagination. Characterizing man as "the writing instrument," he is one who "sits as a contemplator/ In secret frenzies of realization," and he is also the one who "breathes the universe." (Spectacle, Pond, and Hog are islands off the coast of Maine.)

STANLEY KUNITZ

was born in Worcester, Massachusetts, in 1905. His father, a businessman, had committed suicide before his son was born, and his mother opened a dry goods store to repay the family debts. In Worcester High School he edited the school magazine; at Harvard University he was graduated *summa cum laude* and received the Garrison Prize for poetry. Following three years of military service during World War II he was awarded a Guggenheim Fellowship. At forty he became a teacher, invigorating the poetry sessions at such institutions as Yale, Brandeis, Bennington, Columbia, and the University of Washington. He also edited *Twentieth Century Authors*, an important reference work, and the *Yale Series of Younger Poets*.

Kunitz's first volume, *Intellectual Things*, was published when he was twenty-five. After five publishers had turned it down, his *Selected Poems: 1928–1958* appeared when he was in his fifties and was awarded the Pulitzer Prize. *The Testing Tree*, published in his mid-sixties, was the result of ten years' accumulating distinction and it was, wrote Richard Wilbur, "a reassurance as to what poetry can be in these times. There is no limiting oddity of style or attack, but a whole nature eloquently open to the sweetness and anguish of things."

Kunitz reveals an unusual gift for translating physical facts into lyrical-metaphysical ideas and shaping abstractions into firmly organized presentations. Certain critics found Kunitz dense and over-subtle, but only a few of his poems fail to yield a direct and heartfelt meaning. There is, moreover, a moving concern with the problems of his time and a never flinching purpose:

> In a murderous time
> the heart breaks and breaks
> and lives by breaking.
> It is necessary to go
> through dark and deeper dark
> and not to turn.

"The War Against the Trees" (page 63) is both a technical and a meaningful triumph. In a set of loosely rhymed six-line stanzas Kunitz depicts an all-too-common phenomenon of the American scene. It is not merely a feeling of nostalgia that moves the poet to protest against the wreckage wrought by "bulldozers, drunk with gasoline," the ruin that erases a hundred years every time a great tree goes down, but that the ecology of the green world is threatened while the red bulldozers disappear

> Into the suburbs of their grievous age.

"The Portrait" (page 65) is so obviously autobiographical that any comment would be not only superfluous but intrusive.

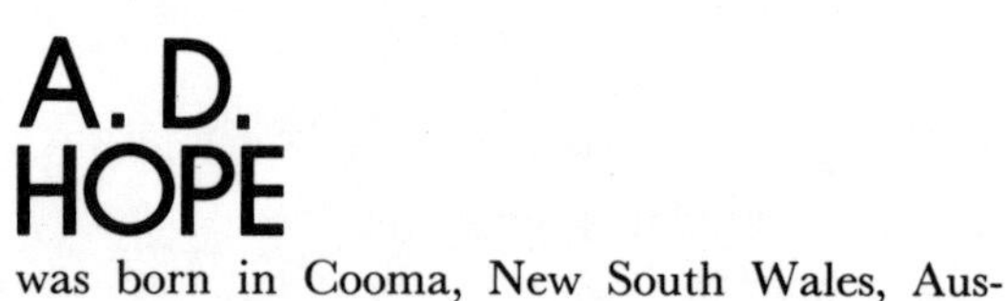

A. D. HOPE

was born in Cooma, New South Wales, Australia, in 1907. He wrote his first book at eight and "an edifying tract" at twelve. He took B.A. degrees at the University of Sydney and the University of Oxford, became a lecturer at the University of Melbourne and Professor of English at the Australian National University, came to America on a grant from the Carnegie Foundation and was co-winner of the 1965 Encyclopaedia Award for Literature.

There is a lot of the finesse of the eighteenth century in Hope's poetry and more than a little of the disillusion and desperateness of the twentieth. Not since Pope have couplets been written so deftly and divertingly; not since Swift has satire been more devastating. Hope's erotic poems are witty as well as warm; he has a way of making the unspeakable not only articulate but also memorable. Rejecting the view that poetry is primarily self-expression, Hope believes that it is "principally concerned to 'express' its subject and in doing so to create an emotion which is the feeling of the poem and not necessarily the feeling of the poet."

Hope's *Collected Poems: 1930–1965* followed by *New Poems: 1965–1969* received unstinted praise. The London *Times* concluded that Hope had established himself as "the kind of presence we associate only with truly formidable talents." The *New York Times* said that his poems "reveal a man in the plenitude of his powers; in range and technical skill in full mastery of his gifts. At least a handful of the poems bear the mark of eternity." There seems no doubt that Hope is the most impressive of Australian poets and also one of the most persuasive poets of his day.

"Imperial Adam" (page 66) is a startling poem which, wrote Thomas Lask, "packs the power of a hundred sermons on original sin. It is not a sermon; it is a splendid poem, but the sermon is there nonetheless." Retelling the story of the Fall, the details take on new and vividly sensual significance. The first cohabitation and the first birth are unashamedly yet quaintly depicted while the pregnant animals attend:

> The gravid elephant, the calving hind,
> The breeding bitch, the she-ape big with young
> Were the first gentle midwives of mankind;
> The teeming lioness rasped her with her tongue.

Classical in form and charming in effect, nothing prepares the reader for the climax of the final stanza and the shock of its dramatic last line.

"The Brides" (page 68) is, in spite of its alluring title, a bitterly ironic poem. Instead of the sweet and tender sentiments accompanying the marriage ceremony, Hope sees the hushed march toward the altar as the product of an assembly line. The comparison of the wedding rites to the automobile industry is cruelly pursued through verse after verse as the bride becomes the much desired high-priced luxury.

> Now slowly through the show-room's flattering glare
> See her wheeled in to love, console, obey,
> Shining and silent! Parson with a prayer
> Blesses the number-plate, she rolls away.

"Moschus Moschiferus" (page 69) is a subtler but no less bitter poem. In the most precise and strictly rhymed quatrains Hope relates how a species of tiny musk-deer is hunted down and killed for only one thing: the glands that hold the marketable scent, while the bodies are left to rot away. The subtitle (*"A Song for St. Cecilia's Day"*) seems incongruous, but it emphasizes the pity—and the terrible irony—of the slaughter of the "most archaic of deer," soon to become extinct. The little animals are lured to their death by flutes that play wavering melodies—and Saint Cecilia is the patron saint of music.

W. H. AUDEN

was born in 1907 in York, in the Midlands of England, son of a medical officer and a nurse. Educated at Christ Church, Oxford, he abandoned a biological scholarship and determined to be a poet. He taught for five years, and spent considerable time abroad: in Germany, where it was said, he searched for God and found Freud; in Spain, where, during the Civil War, he joined the Loyalists; in China, where he collaborated with Christopher Isherwood on *Journey to a War.* In his thirties he came to America and took out citizenship papers. He lived for a while in Ischia, the little volcanic island near Naples, until it grew "too expensive and too touristy," and in his early fifties settled in Kirchstetten, a small Austrian town an hour by train from Vienna. In his mid-sixties he took up residence in Christ Church, Oxford, but continued to spend the summers in Austria.

A fecund creator, Auden was not only the most eloquent but also the most impressive poet of his generation. His 466-page *Collected Poems* was published when he was thirty-eight; it was followed by half a dozen volumes of poetry, one of which, *The Age of Anxiety* (subtitled "A Baroque Eclogue") won the Pulitzer Prize in 1948 and characterized an epoch. Auden was also a prolific critic —his most stimulating essays were collected in *The Dyer's Hand*—

an opera librettist, an anthologist, and compiler of a "commonplace book" *(A Certain World)* which was a sort of offhand literary autobiography.

Much of Auden's early poetry was written in protest against the state of things as they were; the tone was dissident and ambiguous with an air of indefinable menace. Beginning with the poems in *On This Island*, the style simplified and the diction intensified. The imagery suggested a time of disaster as well as an age of anxiety; his was an utterance rich in learning and lyricism. In a deceptively light tone Auden sounded macabre and sinister strains, while deeply ironical notes (as in "Musée des Beaux Arts" and "The Unknown Citizen") were communicated in the most casual tone of voice.

Auden alternately delighted and irritated his admirers with his many-giftedness and the frequency with which he used those gifts to fashion trivialities. But it was also Auden who, according to the London *Times*, "transformed the language of poetry so that it could deal with a vast new range of subjects, appreciating at once their sensual and philosophical aspects."

"Musée des Beaux Arts" (page 71) takes a general observation and brings it to play upon a specific situation. Breughel's painting "The Fall of Icarus" in the Royal Museum in Brussels is a work of art by an Old Master who, as Auden shows, understands the human condition. Turning the picture into a poem, Auden gives the old myth new vitality. The poem, like the painting, derives its force from the contrast between the tragic downfall of the reckless youth and the unperturbed calm of the landscape: the undistracted ploughman busy with his work, and the ship sailing on, everything proceeding as usual amid the universal unconcern.

It is interesting to compare Anne Sexton's treatment of the same subject ("To a Friend whose Work has come to Triumph") on page 189.

"The Unknown Citizen" (page 72) is a flatly satiric portrait of what might be considered the traditional average man, a respectable member of the community who thinks and does what everyone else thinks and does, who holds the properly timed opinions, who accepts every situation unquestioningly, and who has neither the time nor the inclination for self-examination.

"In Memory of W. B. Yeats" (page 74) is one poet's tribute to another. It is not an unreserved eulogy. Auden recalls that in his later years, Yeats distrusted the lower as well as the middle classes, consorted with the rich, feared movements toward a better social order and yearned for an aristocratic system. Half ruefully, half prophetically, Auden says:

> You were silly like us: your gift survived it all;
> The parish of rich women, physical decay,
> Yourself; mad Ireland hurt you into poetry.
> Now Ireland has her madness and her weather still.

The poem approaches the end affirmatively:

> Follow, poet, follow right
> To the bottom of the night,
> With your unconstraining voice
> Still persuade us to rejoice.

It ends majestically:

> In the deserts of the heart
> Let the healing fountain start,
> In the prison of his days
> Teach the free man how to praise.

Kipling's "views" (which Auden says Time has pardoned) were politically bigoted, narrow and jingoistic. Paul Claudel was a French poet, essayist, and diplomat who offended many because of his defiant religious opinions.

In the first line of the next-to-last stanza the word "farming" has sometimes been considered an error and the line has been reprinted as: "With the forming of a verse." This, of course, blunts the point of the image and ruins the succeeding line.

THEODORE ROETHKE

was born in 1908 in Saginaw, Michigan, where his family owned twenty-five flower-growing acres of which a quarter-million feet were under glass. He remembered the greenhouses as a jungle and a paradise. Educated at the University of Michigan and Harvard University, he taught at Lafayette College, Pennsylvania State University (he was the varsity tennis coach at both institutions), at Bennington College and the University of Washington. His career as a poet was spectacularly successful; he received every award a poet can hope to win, including two Guggenheim Fellowships, the Pulitzer Prize, the Bollingen Prize, and the National Book Award.

Differing from his course as a poet, Roethke's personal life was anything but prosperous. A multifaceted manic-depressive, his delicately calibrated and precariously balanced mind made Roethke a victim of constant tensions. He was hospitalized intermittently; he was given shock treatments; he was nursed painstakingly. He never stopped writing; he said he did some of his best work when he felt the oncoming manic phase. He quoted Emily Dickinson's line: "Much madness is divinest sense," and intimated that, like Hart Crane and others, he achieved the highest degree of creativity from induced derangement of the senses. He liked to align himself with such wildly ecstatic poets as Baudelaire and Blake. He died in his fifty-sixth year apparently of a heart attack in a neighbor's swimming pool.

Poetry was Roethke's only therapy. His method was "to think part way through and feel the rest of the way." His imagination was intense; his jangling passions found expression in some of the roughest rhapsodies and some of the most restrained love poems of the period. A few years before his death he wrote: "I have tried to transmute and purify my 'life,' the sense of being defiled by it, in both small and formal and sometimes blunt short poems and, latterly, in longer poems which try to catch the very movement of the mind itself, to trace the spiritual history of the protagonist (not 'I' personally) of all haunted and harried men."

> A man sees, as he dies,
> Death's possibilities;
> My heart sways with the world.
> I am that final thing:
> A man learning to sing.

"Cuttings" (page 77) is one of Roethke's greenhouse poems which illustrate what Kenneth Burke called his "vegetal radicalism." Revived from his early associations with the family flower-raising, the images are both exact and allusive. The coming-to-life of a plant from primeval sources, the "urge, wrestle, resurrection of dry sticks . . . the tight grains parting at last," is symbolic of all birth.

"Elegy for Jane" (page 79), is a tender mourning on the death of a student, a love poem touching and unique. It is in such a poem that Roethke's voice, often blurred and unsure of itself, rings with complete clarity.

"In a Dark Time" (page 80) is one of Roethke's later poems which he labelled "Sequence, Sometimes Metaphysical." In most of his poetry Roethke had abandoned rhyme; yet in the later, darker poems rhyme accentuated the meaning as well as the music. In a searching soliloquy, the poet relates to all things in nature—"beasts of the hill and serpents of the den . . . a night flowing with birds, a ragged moon . . . all natural shapes blazing unnatural light"—and finds out what he is. A fallen fear-ridden man, he climbs out of his fear.

> The mind enters itself, and God the mind,
> The one is One, free in the tearing wind.

STEPHEN SPENDER

was born in 1909 in London of mixed English, German, and Jewish descent. His parents died during his boyhood and, at fifteen, he came under "one of the most important influences of my life, that of my maternal grandmother, Hilda Schuster. She was extremely influenced by a wish to share an experience of something 'new' and modern with me, her most isolated grandson who most needed her. . . . I grew up in an atmosphere of belief in progress curiously mixed with apprehension." As a child he thought of being a painter; at seventeen he tried to support himself by printing chemists' labels; at nineteen he set up on his own press a paperbound pamphlet of his first poems, *Nine Experiments*. He attended University College, Oxford, where he joined a circle of poets, notably W. H. Auden, Louis MacNeice, and C. Day Lewis who was to become (in 1968) Poet Laureate. He joined the Communist party but, resenting regimentation, soon repudiated it. Details of the period are chronicled in his autobiographical *The God that Failed* and *World Within World*.

Much of Spender's poetry focuses on the materials of everyday, on the aspects and functions of modern technology. An early poem, "The Landscape Near an Aerodrome," begins:

> More beautiful and soft than any moth
> With burring furred antennae feeling its huge path

Through dusk, the air-liner with shut-off engine
Glides over suburbs and the sleeves set trailing tall
To point the wind.

Spender believed what Hart Crane maintained: that unless modern poetry can "absorb the machine, acclimatize it as naturally and casually as trees, cattle, galleons, castles, and all other associations of the past, then poetry has failed of its full contemporary function." In Spender's words, modern poetry must employ technological symbols as easily as "*rose* and *love* in a forgotten rhyme."

Spender has often been compared to Shelley, and it is sometimes hard to determine where ecstasy ends and rhetorical exhortation begins, but the best of Spender is buoyed up by an immediacy of response and an unmistakably passionate involvement. "Drink from here energy," he writes in "Not Palaces," demanding complete physical and spiritual participation:

Eye, gazelle, delicate wanderer,
Drinker of horizon's fluid line;
Ear that suspends on a chord
The spirit drinking timelessness;
Touch, love, all senses . . .

Energy and a nerve-sensitive dynamism give Spender's poetry its distinction; a tense drive toward exploration gives it its force.

"An Elementary Classroom in a Slum" (page 81) contrasts the grandeur of poetry symbolized by a bust of Shakespeare ("civilized dome riding all cities") and the beauty of nature, as exemplified by travel posters ("belled, flowery, Tyrolese valley"), with the ugliness of the children's surroundings ("a narrow street sealed in with a lead sky"), a world of illness, poverty, and exploitation. The poet appeals to those in power:

Break, O break open, till they break the town
And show the children to the fields, and all their world

Azure on their sands, to let their tongues
Run naked into books, the white and green leaves open
The history theirs whose language is the sun.

"The Truly Great" (page 83) celebrates the pioneers, the unsung champions, the visionaries inflamed with a burning belief in humanity. It is the firebringers, children of light—"born of the sun"—who never allow "the traffic to smother the flowering of the spirit," who bring light out of darkness, faith out of confusion, and who, in their lives fight for life. They are the truly great who leave "the vivid air signed with their honor."

ELIZABETH BISHOP

was born in 1911 in Worcester, Massachusetts, was graduated from Vassar College, and has traveled widely. Part of her childhood was spent in Nova Scotia; later she lived in Key West, after which she divided her time between the United States and Brazil. It has been said that she blended New England severity with tropical floridity. In 1955 she was awarded the Pulitzer Prize for the combined edition of *North & South* and *A Cold Spring*; in 1969 her *Complete Poems* gathered the work of thirty years and received the National Book Award. She is also co-editor of *An Anthology of Twentieth Century Brazilian Poetry.*

Miss Bishop's technique is that of the impressionists, a stroke here, a line there. The visual effects are both precise and suggestive, a trait which she shares with Marianne Moore, one of her first appreciators. "At last," wrote Marianne Moore, "we have someone who knows and who is not didactic." Fantastic yet factual, Elizabeth Bishop discloses the unusual aspects of reality without being a surrealist; in her own words she gives the reader "glimpses of the always-more-successful surrealism of everyday life." For example:

> Along the street below
> The water-wagon comes

throwing its hissing snowy fan across
peelings and newspapers. The water dries
light-dry, dark-wet, the pattern
of the cool watermelon.

A detail on a map prompts this odd but exact image:

These peninsulas take the water between thumb and finger
Like women feeling for the smoothness of yard-goods.

A cock crowing "with horrible insistence"

grates like a wet match
from the broccoli patch,
flares, and all over town begins to catch.

If poetry, like music (as defined by Berlioz) is "the art of producing emotion," Elizabeth Bishop fulfills her function as poet by evoking, even in such technical exercises as the sestinas "A Miracle for Breakfast" and "September rain falls on the house," an immediate emotional response from the reader.

"The Prodigal" (page 84) is a new treatment of the story of the son "who wasted his substance with riotous living" (Luke 15: 11–32) and was sent into the fields to feed swine. Using a flexible arrangement of rhymes, the poet presents a picture which is both realistic and fanciful, vivid and grimly comic.

"Florida" (page 85) is a succession of witty images. "Tanagers embarrassed by their flashiness," "pelicans whose delight it is to clown," "mosquitoes go hunting to the tune of their ferocious obbligatos," "fireflies map the heavens in the marsh." The brilliance touches almost every line. It toys with the quaintly named sea shells, through one of which the alligator "whimpers," and its exuberance justifies itself in praise of "the state with the prettiest name."

"The Armadillo" (page 87) is only incidentally about the little bony-plated mammal, yet the relation between the fire balloon and the small armor-clad creature hunched like "a weak mailed fist" is delicately established. The poem is dedicated to Robert Lowell, who wrote that Miss Bishop has "a humorous, commanding genius for picking up the unnoticed, now making something sprightly and right, and now a great monument. . . . When we read her, we enter the classical serenity of a new country."

MURIEL RUKEYSER

was born in 1913 in New York City. She entered Vassar College and left it after two years to attend sessions at Columbia University. She worked her way through the ground course at Roosevelt Aviation School but was not allowed to pilot a plane because her parents refused to sign a contract permitting a minor to fly. It was at this time that she wrote her first important poem, which became the title-poem of her first book, *Theory of Flight*, issued when she was twenty-one.

Since that time she has published a dozen books of poems; *The Life of Poetry*, a critical volume, speaking for the interrelation of poetry and other disciplines, including science; a biography of the scientist Willard Gibbs; *The Traces of Thomas Hariot*, a re-creation of the almost forgotten Elizabethan explorer, philosopher, and astronomer; *The Orgy*, a ritual celebration in rollicking prose; as well as books for children. She has translated Octavio Paz, the Mexican poet, and has taught groups ranging from two-year-olds to college students and teachers.

When Muriel Rukeyser's first book appeared, her dramatic power and her gift for excitement were quickly recognized. The intensity of her poems was felt even before they were fully understood; the meaning, sometimes muffled by the rush of thought, declared itself in impulsive and often hurtling emotion. Her later work achieved a new definiteness as well as a greater depth. The temper rather than the technique of her work makes it affecting;

it is uplifted by a passion which, freeing itself from self, is born of compassion.

"Effort at Speech between Two People" (page 89) is one of her dramatic early poems. An almost painful monologue, it is an extraordinary expression: a disclosure of autobiographical glimpses surrounding a passionate appeal for communication. The thrust of feeling is subdued but it is strong, quiet and compelling.

"Boy with his Hair Cut Short" (page 91) is a poem prompted by a period of depression and social unrest. The details are starkly pictorial—the cheerless room with the overstuffed sofa, the drugstore neon sign, the solicitous sister "simple in blue." But it is the sense of anxiety, the need of finding work, the newly pressed suit laid out, the carfare on the shelf, "the blue vein . . . pitifully beating," that move the reader with its undercurrent of tenderness and pathos.

"Bringing" (page 92) is an unrhymed but deeply rhythmed hymn of praise, an exaltation of the young who "offer their open faces . . . offer their bodies . . . offer their hands." The poet eloquently hails those who resist not only wars but rewards,

> Bringing their life entire   they come to this moment
> Bringing their life entire   they come to this place

RANDALL JARRELL

was born in 1914 in Nashville, Tennessee. Graduated from Vanderbilt University, he taught at various institutions until he settled in Greensboro, North Carolina, where he was Professor of English at the Woman's College of North Carolina. He was literary editor of *The Nation*, poetry critic for other publications and, for two years, Consultant in Poetry at the Library of Congress. During World War II he spent three years with the Army Air Force in the Pacific and as an operator-trainer in Arizona. He was fifty-one when he died after being struck by an automobile on a dark road in the woods. A memorial volume of assessments by twenty-eight distinguished contributors appeared two years after his death.

A protean creator, Jarrell was the author of seven volumes of poetry, one of which, *The Woman at the Washington Zoo*, won the National Book Award; a coruscating novel, *Pictures from an Exhibition*, which was a satire on university life; a catalytic book of criticism, *Poetry and the Age*; a translation of Goethe's *Faust*; and several books for young people, notably *The Bat-Poet* and *The Animal Family*.

Poets were quick to praise Jarrell equally as poet and critic. Reviewing *Poetry and the Age* Delmore Schwartz wrote that Jarrell succeeds "in being joyous, angry, contemptuous, and gay, as well as lucid, direct, and colloquial with complete genuineness and ease." Robert Lowell said that "his gifts, both by nature and by a lifetime of hard dedication and growth, were wit, pathos, and brilliance of intelligence. These qualities, dazzling in themselves, were often so well employed that he became, I think, the most heartbreaking English poet of his generation." Robert Watson spoke of his integrity as an appraiser: "If God were a writer and wrote a book that Randall did not think was good, Randall would not have hesitated to give it a bad review. And if God complained, Randall would then set about showing God what was wrong with his sentences."

Jarrell's criticisms were often barbed, witty and cruel. He disposed of a mediocre versifier by saying that he was "writing poems that might have been written *by* a typewriter *on* a typewriter." He characterized an academic scholar by asking "What can be more tedious than a man whose every sentence is a balanced epigram without wit, profundity, or taste?" "Tomorrow morning," he commented wryly, "some poet may, like Byron, wake up to find himself famous for having written a sensational novel, or for having killed his wife—but it will not be for having written a poem."

Perhaps the best summary of Jarrell was made by Denis Donoghue, critic and teacher at University College in Dublin: "Reading his poems is like the relief of breaking a wounded silence, letting the pain drain away in words, in companionable talk. When we say his idiom is conversational, we mean that it is like the conversation that helps in trouble; balm to hurt minds."

For "The Death of the Ball Turret Gunner" (page 93) Jarrell furnished this note: "A ball turret was a plexiglass sphere set into the belly of a B-17 or B-24, and inhabited by two .50 caliber machine-guns and one man, a short small man. When this gunner tracked with his machine-guns a fighter attacking his bomber from below, he revolved with the turret; hunched upside-down in his little sphere, he looked like the foetus in the womb. The fighters which attacked him were armed with cannon-firing explosive shells. The hose was a steam hose."

"90 North" (page 94) is a chilling fantasy, and it is also a double portrait of the mature poet who imagines a bitter journey to the extreme north and the boy who has a heroic dream of going to the North Pole. Dramatic and desperate throughout, the poem builds toward its frightening conclusion that out of the ignorant darkness "nothing comes from nothing," and reaches its unhappy climax in two abrupt lines.

"The Woman at the Washington Zoo" (page 96) is considered one of Jarrell's most penetrating and most revealing poems. The colorfully exotic opening—"The saris go by me from the embassies"—is contrasted with the "dull null navy" suit of the government clerk who, watching, sees a relation between herself and the trapped animals. She is lonelier than the wild beasts—"the world goes by my cage and never sees me"—even the animals do not notice her. Yet, as Stanley Kunitz points out, "just when we are ready to turn away, Jarrell does something magical and triumphant with his woman at the zoo. He has her cry out, addressing the predatory bird who is the figure of lover-death, such words of shameless agony that the despair is transmuted into a fierce exaltation, as the true colors of the world, terrible though they may be, pour back into the poem."

JOHN BERRYMAN

was born in 1914 in McAlester, Oklahoma. Educated at Columbia College and Clare College, Cambridge, England, he taught literature at Wayne University, Detroit, as well as at Harvard, Princeton, and the University of Minnesota. He was in his late twenties when his first book, *Poems*, appeared; it was followed a few years later by the more individualistic *The Dispossessed.* His *Homage to Mistress Bradstreet* (the remarkable seventeenth-century colonial poet) was considered his masterpiece; Edmund Wilson wrote that it was "the most distinguished long poem by an American since *The Waste Land.*" His *77 Dream Songs*, which was awarded the Pulitzer Prize in 1965, was expanded into the 385 poems of *His Toy, His Dream, His Rest*, which won the National Book Award in 1969. The success of these volumes encouraged the publishers to issue earlier work by Berryman, including *Berryman's Sonnets* and *Short Poems.*

The success also had the unfortunate result of unsettling the poet. His style became increasingly singular and anti-poetic. He drank heavily, was often taken to a detoxification center for treatment, and in his fifty-eighth year committed suicide by jumping off a bridge over the Mississippi River in Minnesota. One of the poems in his posthumous volume, *Delusions*, was entitled "Walking into the River."

"Life, friends, is boring" (page 98) is one of the *Dream Songs.*

Eliot had asserted that good poetry can be enjoyed even before it is understood. In "Dream Song—366" Berryman told the reader

> These Songs are not meant to be understood, you understand.
> They are only meant to terrify & comfort.

However, the meaning of "Life, friends, is boring," which is number 14 of the *Dream Songs,* is clear and the expression is candid. The "Henry" who, along with everything else, bores the poet, is (in Berryman's own words) "an imaginary character, a white American in early middle age sometimes in blackface, who has suffered an irreversible loss and talks about himself, sometimes in the first person, sometimes in the third, sometimes even in the second."

"Today is it? Is it today? I shudder" (page 99) is another evidence of Berryman's virtuosity. It is a sonnet in the classical manner, yet it conveys his distinctive idiom. Written in his thirties, *Berryman's Sonnets* record a sometimes happy, sometimes painful love affair. Berryman gives an old rhetoric a new twist. The conceits, the figures of speech, are both romantic and realistic; the yearning of the lover is expressed in a curious nuance, a simile that compares the long awaited advent of the beloved to the impact of a power-driven subway train.

> As the undergrounds piston a force of air
> Before their crash into the station, you
> Are felt before your coming, and the platforms shake.

BARBARA HOWES

was born in 1914 in Boston, where she was brought up. Graduated from Bennington College, she edited *Chimera*, a literary quarterly, and published her first book of poetry, *The Undersea Farmer* in 1948. It was followed by three volumes of poems and various awards. After spending much time abroad—in Italy, France, and Haiti—she made her home with her two sons in North Pownal, Vermont, where, she says, her "hobbies seem to consist mainly of the exactions of the day."

Besides her poetry, she has edited collections of short stories, notably *From the Green Antilles: Writings of the Caribbean* and, with one of her sons, *The Sea-Green Horse: Stories for Young People*. In 1971 she received an award from the National Institute of Arts and Letters for her fusion of sensitivity and sharp-edged expressiveness. The impact of a seventeenth-century poet with a twentieth-century mind is immediately apparent in *The Blue Garden* which appeared in 1972.

"The Gallery" (page 100) is an epitome of Barbara Howes' quality: images that are quiet but convincing, lines that are graceful but firm. The occasional, seemingly haphazard rhymes and the captured ambience—"nothing alive/But painting"—make an effective projection.

"Talking to Animals" (page 101) is a whimsical but perceptive piece of writing. It is not only pet-owners who know that making oneself understood to animals

—as to people—
Is a question of tone of voice.

A "hogan" is a house built of earth-walls supported by timbers, the traditional dwelling of the Navaho Indians.

DYLAN THOMAS

was born in 1914 in the Welsh seaport town of Swansea. Son of a schoolteacher, he had little formal schooling, but (as evidenced in his poetry) was brought up on Welsh folklore. After attending the local grammar school he became a reporter, a documentary film script writer, and a reader of poetry for the British Broadcasting Corporation. He was wretchedly poor most of his life until, toward the end, he came to the United States and gave recitals in crowded halls and at more than forty universities. No one who heard him read poetry—his own or others—ever forgot the hypnotic quality, half-declamation, half-chant, of his voice.

Sensationally successful, Thomas felt at home in America. "I don't believe in New York," he said, "but I love Third Avenue." There were many parties at which he drank heavily; he went habitually from bar to bar. A manic-depressive, he entertained his quickly-made friends with imaginary lectures on such topics as "A Typical Day in My Welsh Bog" and "A Bard's-Eye View of New York by a Dollar-Mad Nightingale." At thirty-five he described himself mockingly as "old, small, dark, and darting-doting-eyed, balding and toothlessing." On his third visit to America he celebrated his thirty-ninth birthday in New York. The reckless festivities ended in sudden illness and a total collapse. Taken to a hospital, he died two weeks later.

Thomas was twenty when his first book, *Eighteen Poems*, was published. It startled readers with its strange word magic and its driving force. Superabundant vigor and a childlike, almost irresponsible delight in turmoil were emphasized in his second book, *Twenty-Five Poems*, published when he was twenty-two. The image-crowded lines in his *Collected Poems* effect something between highly charged sexual energy and exuberant innocence. Edith Sitwell wrote that their spirit was "that of the beginning of creative things. From the depths of being, from the roots of the world, a voice speaks."

Thomas' last work, *Under Milk Wood*, written shortly before his death, was tried out in New York with the poet reading two of the parts. A cross between a play and a pageant, ranging from lyrical meditations to bawdy ballads which project the essence of a community, it has been countlessly performed. Besides this transfiguration of the coastal town in which he lived, and his other poetry, Thomas wrote several volumes of short stories. One of them *(Quite Early One Morning)* contains the immensely popular "A Child's Christmas in Wales," which Thomas recorded and whose perennial charm has been compared to Dickens' "A Christmas Carol."

"Fern Hill" (page 103) carries the reader along on wave after wave of lively, childhood irresponsibilities. It is a backward flight into a time that lets the boy

> play and be
> Golden in the mercy of his means.

Image follows image with a spontaneity that stirs the mind and insinuates itself into the heart.

"Do Not Go Gentle into that Good Night" (page 105) is a poetic paradox, formal yet fluent. A most moving tribute to his father, it is put into the confines of a villanelle, proving that the strictest form can be infused with deeply felt poignance. It is interesting to compare the measured solemnity of this elegiac set of tercets with Cummings' "my father moved through dooms of love" on page 49.

JOHN MALCOLM BRINNIN

was born in 1916 in Halifax, Nova Scotia, of American parents, brought up in Detroit and educated at the University of Michigan and at Harvard University. A gifted communicator, he taught at Vassar College and the University of Connecticut, and, in 1961, succeeded Robert Lowell in the teaching of poetry at Boston University. A tireless traveler, he made twenty-five trips to Europe, including two to the Soviet Union, and almost as many to Africa, Central and South America. His preoccupation with travel led to *The Sway of the Grand Saloon,* a memorial biography which is also a highly informative history of North Atlantic ship-crossings and the great ocean liners.

Brinnin has also written a distinguished memoir, *Dylan Thomas in America*, an intimate, tender yet unsparing portrayal of the Welsh poet, and *The Third Rose: Gertrude Stein and Her World*, an authoritative work on that controversial figure. As a non-academic stimulator of poetry, he directed the Poetry Center of the New York YM-YWHA for seven years. With Bill Reed he skillfully edited a comprehensive anthology, *Twentieth Century Poetry*.

Brinnin's first publication, *The Garden is Political*, which appeared in his twenty-sixth year, was followed by five other volumes of poetry, including a representative *Selected Poems*. He said he knew that "you don't write a poem until there's a poem to write; you have to be urged from inside;" and the poems Brinnin has written are urgent. They range from childhood reminiscences to philosophical speculations, from political documents to parodies.

"Nuns at Eve" (page 106) is one of Brinnin's lighter poems. With instinctive taste and touches of humor he illumines the picture of the softball-playing sisters. A delightful detail:

> . . . the obliging sun
> Dazzling the pitcher's box
> With a last celestial light upon
> The gold-spiked halo of the Virgin in her niche,
> Leads Sister Mary John to a wild pitch.

"The Ascension: 1925" (page 108) is a strictly fashioned sonnet in which the poet in his forties remembers how, when he was nine years old, he stood watching the balloon

> As, nuzzling upward from her stake, she rose
> In strict submission to the absolute.

"Grave Mind I Loved" (page 109) is a punning parody. The first line is a take-off on a once popular lyric, "Pale hands I loved," as well as a play on the word "grave." The last line, bringing together the two Johns, Brinnin and Donne, recalls Donne's unhappy message to his mother when he was imprisoned for eloping with his patron's niece, Anne Moore: "John Donne—Anne Donne—Undone."

"Skin Diving in the Virgins" (page 110) is not, as it may seem, another play on words. It is a colorful reminiscence of a vacation in the semi-tropical Virgin Islands. The associations—the drink-dispenser and the sunken vessel, "like Alfonso, somewhat Spanish in the stern"; the pelicans, "crazy old men in baseball caps"; the upright barracuda—are as witty as they are vivid.

GWENDOLYN BROOKS

born in 1917 in Topeka, Kansas, married, and moved to Chicago, Illinois. She wrote poetry as a child; at fourteen she saw her first work in print. Her professional career began with publication in *Poetry* when she was twenty-eight. Her first book, *A Street in Bronzeville*, was a quiet but haunting evocation. J. Saunders Redding wrote that Gwendolyn Brooks "gives the exact pitch to the undertones of Negro life without resorting to the obvious device of ringing the brazen bell of dialect." Her second book, *Annie Allen*, won the Pulitzer Prize in 1950 for its distinguished portrayal of one woman whose environment is a place called Bronzeville. Besides the Pulitzer Prize, she won various workshop awards, two Guggenheim Fellowships, and grants from the American Academy of Arts and Letters and the National Institute of Arts and Letters. *The World of Gwendolyn Brooks*, an anthology of her work from 1945 to 1968, appeared in her mid-fifties.

Her poetry continued to speak meaningfully to black people about their lives everywhere, to Afro-Americans on street corners and in colleges. "I went with young poets to a bar," she related. "They read their poetry, and the response was tremendous. I want to be able to do that."

"the rites for Cousin Vit" (page 112) and "manicure" (page 113), from *Annie Allen*, have a common background and a common manner, but they are widely different in form. The first is a sonnet, colloquial in tone but precise in technique, a disillusioned, half-defiant, completely vitalized portrait.

"manicure" is another kind of portrayal. The picture of the manicurist and her customer who is confident that "this yellow, mellow bit is buyable" is insinuating and incisive.

"We Real Cool" (page 114), from *The Bean Eaters*, is a savage vignette from the world of general confusion and private terror that Gwendolyn Brooks knows so well, a world where the struggle to survive is a daily desperation. The despair, disguised as a careless shrug, is dramatized in the brusque, painfully tense lines.

was born in 1917 in Boston, Massachusetts. His was a famous family; it included the nineteenth century poet James Russell Lowell, who was also an ambassador to England; Amy Lowell, an experimental twentieth century poet; and Lawrence Lowell, president of Harvard. After being graduated from St. Mark's Preparatory School, Robert Lowell attended Harvard for two years, but transferred to Kenyon College because the poet-critic John Crowe Ransom was there teaching a new generation of poets.

For a while Lowell supported himself by teaching and working in a New York publishing concern. During World War II he became a conscientious objector and was sentenced to a year in prison, but was released after five months. His first book, *Land of Unlikeness* had been published in his twenty-seventh year; his second volume, *Lord Weary's Castle*, which appeared two years later, won the Pulitzer Prize. Critics recognized that a poet of unusual stature had arrived, one who combined rebellion and tradition, formalism and experiment. It was apparent that he had achieved something like a disciplined wildness, bold in image, powerful yet controlled in thought.

Succeeding volumes established Lowell as the most important younger poet of the period. Awards, fellowships, and grants succeeded each other. His *Life Studies* won the National Book Award in 1960 for its accurate observation and soaring imagination. "Poetry of this order," wrote the English critic A. Alvarez, "needs neither to be justified or explained. One should simply be thankful that there is still someone able to write it."

In his forties Lowell began writing for the theatre. *The Old Glory*, consisting of three one-act plays, was successfully produced off Broadway. He also made free adaptations of Racine's *Phèdre* and Aeschylus' *Prometheus Bound*, reestablishing the union of drama and poetry. His paraphrases from the classic Greek to modern Russian were collected in *Imitations*, versions that, in spite of the modest title, are recreated poems rather than literal renderings.

For the Union Dead, generally considered the most impassioned volume he had yet published, was acclaimed for its fusion of violence and beauty. *Near the Ocean* contained only thirteen poems, some of them among Lowell's darkest meditations. *Notebook: 1967–1968* was composed of some two hundred and sixty sonnets, mostly unrhymed, and presented intimate portraits of himself and his family, social criticism, and private associations. It earned Lowell the title of "Leader of the Confessional School" and extended his freedom of communication. Altogether, Lowell's poetry was a poetry fierce in its tensions, fiercer in its protests, protests not only against crass industrialism, corruption, and war, but also against the apathy of the age.

Three full-scale biographical and critical studies examined the private, self-scrutinizing ("confessional") poet and the public man: *Robert Lowell: The First Twenty Years* by Hugh B. Staples; *Robert Lowell: A Portrait of the Artist in his Time*, edited by Michael London and Robert Boyers; and *The Public Poetry of Robert Lowell* by Patrick Cosgrave.

In "For the Union Dead" (page 115) Lowell contrasts the memories of his youth in Boston with the present scene—the aquarium he remembers fades into a stream of "giant finned cars" that

nose forward like fish:
a savage servility
slides by on grease.

The poem centers about St. Gauden's Civil War Relief memorializing Colonel Robert Gould Shaw and his troops, the bronze "bell-cheeked Negro infantry." The Latin motto, *Relinquunt omnia servare rem publicam*, ("They leave everything to serve the republic") is an adaptation of the inscription on the memorial. An elegy for the Union dead develops into a lament for the materialism, the cruelty ("the drained faces of Negro school-children"), and the accepted horror (a photograph of Hiroshima advertising a commercial product) which characterizes the apathy of the age.

"Skunk Hour" (page 118), dedicated to Elizabeth Bishop, has something of her sharp, exact contemporaneity. Grimly ironic, Lowell assembles an odd lot of people—a hermit heiress, a luckless millionaire, a homosexual decorator—typical of the deterioration of the New England tradition. Then, turning eccentricity into suffering, he reveals his own malaise: "my mind's not right." The sight of a mother skunk and her column of kittens searching for food is a logical, naturalistic end of an understated, unhappy soliloquy.

"Man and Wife" (page 120) is an intensely personal declaration, something that Lowell has rarely written: a ruefully tender love poem. The reference to "the Rahvs in the heat of Greenwich Village" is to Philip Rahv, the American critic, editor, and author of *Image and Idea*, a collection of clarifying critical essays. *Miltown* is a tranquilizer.

WILLIAM JAY SMITH

was born in 1918 in Winnfield, Louisiana, a town which his father's family had helped to found. On his mother's side he is (he states explicitly) one-sixteenth Cherokee. He served in World War II as Navy personnel and liaison officer and followed his studies at Columbia University as a Rhodes Scholar at Oxford. After teaching at Columbia he was poet-in-residence at Williams College, Professor of English at Hollins, and, for two years, Consultant in Poetry to the Library of Congress.

Recipient of numerous awards, including a Ford Foundation theater grant, Smith has an unusually versatile mind and manner. He has written several books for children, has translated the writings of Jules Laforgue, is the author of a literary curiosity *(The Spectra Hoax)*, and has invented various typographical oddities. As a poet he is an uncommonly adept craftsman. Stanley Kunitz wrote that he "ranges without loss of equilibrium from light verse to poems of reflection, love, and anger." His *New and Selected Poems*, including the best from four previously published volumes, appeared in 1970.

"Rear Vision" (page 121) begins with a whimsicality, turns metaphysical, and ends in a macabre speculation. Here the craftsman and the creator are indissolubly combined.

"Hull Bay, St. Thomas" (page 122) is composed in Smith's later manner. Discarding the rhymes and regular rhythms which he had hitherto favored, Smith employs free verse to disclose a happy occasion and an increasingly colorful scene. The images—"gun-gray gunwales like exhausted birds," "pelicans with ludicrous long beaks like tilted shears," "the sun, askew, a blob of red quickly cut from Christmas paper"—are particularly vivid.

MAY SWENSON

was born in 1919 in Logan, Utah, the first of ten children of immigrant Swedish parents. After graduating from Utah State University, she came to New York, the principal scene of her career. She was, for a time, an editor as well as a judge for the Academy of American Poets and the National Book Award. She received a Guggenheim Fellowship and grants from the National Institute of Arts and Letters and the Ford Foundation. Her experimental play, *The Floor*, was produced in 1966.

Quick to transform the ordinary scene into intensities of observation and images of pure vision, she evinced a novelty of language in everything she touched. "Poetry," she wrote, "must do more than interpret the particularities of existence or the experience of the poet's own generation and environment. It must also speak to and for every age. Its material should be such that a savage would have found it familiar, and such that Neo-Man a thousand years from now may say 'Yes, I have felt this, too.' The fact that our present civilization seems sealed and smothered in synthetic wrappings makes it only the more imperative for poetry to insist with all its strength on uttering the elemental."

Half Sun, Half Sleep, her fifth volume, justified what she had written about poetry and received renewed praise. Reviewing the book, Karl Shapiro wrote, "It hardly matters what her subject is.

Her concentration on the verbal equivalent of experience is so true, so often brilliant, that one watches her with hope and pleasure." Critics united to call attention to her free-roaming imagination and verbal inventiveness, her word-plays, games, riddles—she composed a book for children entitled *Poems to Solve*—iconographs, and calligraphic designs. Whatever her method, simple or surrealistic, it is governed by a logic of expression and emotion.

"The Lightning" (page 124) is one of her word-play poems. Using a neat typographical device to indicate the flash, she is roused into considering "a symbol for conceiving the universe," and a chain of communications emanating from all of nature, from cats to kinglets, feathers and flowers.

"Trinity Churchyard, Spring" (page 125) exemplifies May Swenson's power of intensifying a scene with freshness and, even in a churchyard, with delight. The details are assimilated with precision and something like natural magic.

"Sun" (page 127), one of the few poems where Miss Swenson indulges in rhyme, is one of her most graphic evocations. Image after image, one more brilliant than the other—the sun with its "masculine stride," "the unobstructed parapet of noon-blue," the "disciplined planets/ . . . that imitate your stamping feet/in the elliptic dance of fire," "one-sided shield turned to the urgent tide"—mount to a triumphant conclusion:

> divine and glistering your beard with dewy flames
> sprinting to the pantheon and your god-like games.

"The Thickening Mat" (page 129) is a forthright yet imaginative account of a city walk in windswept snow.

RICHARD WILBUR

was born in 1921 in New York City. His forebears were artists, publishers, and editors; it was only natural that Wilbur became editor of the college paper when he attended Amherst College. During World War II he served in the 36th Infantry Division, after which he taught at Harvard and Wellesley and was appointed Professor of English at Wesleyan University.

Nearing fifty, Wilbur was the editor of three works of appraisal; writer of lyrics for the Hellman-Bernstein musical version of *Candide*; author of five books of poetry, one of which *(Things of This World)* was a triple award winner: the Pulitzer Prize, the National Book Award, and the Edna St. Vincent Millay Memorial Award. His renderings of the strict couplets of *The Misanthrope*, *Tartuffe*, and *The School for Wives* were delicate in touch and brilliant in technique. "A large part of the reason for the Molière revival in North America," wrote Clive Barnes, "is the excellence of Richard Wilbur's new translations." John Simon added to the general applause: "Molière is fortunate in having the poet Richard Wilbur as—not translator, too weak a word—but re-creator. Not since Congreve has stage English had such perfectly fused neatness and panache, and even Congreve could manage it only in prose."

Wilbur's own poetry displays the efflorescent images and inventiveness of a virtuoso. Although designed in definite patterns, the lines are full of fresh vitality; the taste is immaculate and the choice of form and phrase unerring. The ease and grace are so apparent that they sometimes conceal a depth of feeling. To those who complained that his poems were often too rigorously structured, too confined in form, Wilbur replied that "the strength of the genie comes of his being confined in a bottle."

"Advice to a Prophet" (page 130) is a half-ironic, half-angry rebuke to dealers in doom, predictors of a worldless mankind. Gravely it speaks for all those who refuse to be scared with talk about the death of the race. Here wit and vision are joined. (Xanthus, capital of ancient Lycia, was twice destroyed.)

In "Digging for China" (page 132) Wilbur turns from protest to playfulness. A childhood reminiscence, it delights with its whimsicality, the dream of "a place where nothing was the same," a place with a different sky and nothing like anything the boy had known, definitely "nothing like New Jersey."

"The Writer" (page 133) again reveals Wilbur's sureness of touch, an expression fine but not finicky. With outspoken love the poem balances on two images. The image of the daughter starting out on a career suggests that of a shipboard voyage—"a commotion of typewriter-keys/ Like a chain hauled over a gunwale," "the stuff of her life is a great cargo," "I wish her a lucky passage." The desire to escape through writing prompts the second image: a trapped starling, an "iridescent creature," struggling to clear "the sill of the world." The relation of the two images is never stated, but subtly, tenderly, implied.

MONA VAN DUYN

was born in 1921 in Waterloo, Iowa, and taught at Iowa University and the University of Louisville. She helped found *Perspectives: A Quarterly of Literature and the Arts* and moved to St. Louis. Her first book, *Valentines to the Wide World*, was published in a limited edition; eight of its poems were reprinted in *A Time of Bees*. Her third volume, *To See, To Take*, received the National Book Award for poetry in 1971 and was also co-winner of the 1971 Bollingen Prize.

Mona Van Duyn has a way of transmuting common things and ordinary experiences into far from ordinary poems of wit and warmth. Hers is a curiously domestic poetry in which the satisfactions and frustrations of domesticity are balanced with grace and humor. "I believe that good poetry can be as ornate as a cathedral or as bare as a pottingshed as long as it confronts the self with honesty and fullness," she wrote. "I find my richest hunting ground for poems in that place where the undomesticated feelings, snapping and snarling, run around the domestic ring. I find myself most interested in the self-definitions which occur in the 'home-base' from which we go out into work, war, politics, and the conquest of nature, and to which we inevitably and constantly return."

"A Sentimental Delusion" (page 135) is a love poem that

could not have been written in any other time but now. Impassioned and fearful—the suspended half-rhymes add to the suspense—the poem pits the lovers, creatures "of pulse and gland," against the menace of machinery, "claiming our consciousness with clank and whirr." Quietly yet reassuringly the poet considers the mechanization of mankind:

> Watt after watt compels us in our kiss,
> and men, whose soft veins harden, envy us
> our burning circuits, our immortal stress.

"An Annual and Perennial Problem" (page 137) is a dexterously playful poem in which the title itself is a play on words. Here the poet uses assonance and half-rhyme to accentuate the botanical "facts" and the very personal bantering tone.

"Homework" (page 139) is a triumph of beauty and badinage. The act of pickling peaches and putting them in the refrigerator is, in every sense, a work of preservation, complete with puns—"there in a frieze they stand"—as the meticulous poet ("a sweating Proust of the pantry shelves") cupboards her product and her poem "in Time's despite."

JAMES DICKEY

was born in 1923 in Atlanta, Georgia. Before he was recognized as a poet, he had a variety of careers. He was a star college athlete, excelling in football and hurdle racing; a night fighter pilot with more than a hundred missions in World War II and Korea; a natural woodsman; an advertising executive; a teacher; a poetry consultant at the Library of Congress; and a lecturer who was also a popular platform personality.

Three volumes of Dickey's poetry had been published before *Buckdancer's Choice* won the National Book Award in 1966. It was followed a year later by *Poems: 1957–1967*, a selection of his previously published books plus a score of new poems. Besides his poetry, Dickey appeared as critic with *Babel to Byzantium*, a less than generous consideration of today's poets, and *Sorties*, in which he dismissed most of his contemporaries—Richard Wilbur is too "neat," Elizabeth Bishop is too "offhand," etc. Far more successful was his novel, *Deliverance*, an apotheosis of virility, a brutal tale in which men not only rape each other but hunt one another down like animals.

Dickey's prime quality is gusto, a seemingly inexhaustible energy that impels and sometimes overwhelms his subjects. His is a ready, even eager, response to violence; it is as if he were glad to be challenged to vehement action. He is at his best when he deals with physical situations that range from the tense to the terrifying, and deals with them in a style that is appropriate: variably long lines with internal spaces to increase tension.

"The Firebombing" (page 140) effectively uses a flashback technique to juxtapose past and present. The poet, "twenty years overweight," is seen eating a snack in his "half-paid-for pantry" in the suburbs:

> Where the lawn mower rests on its laurels
> Where the diet exists
> For my own good   where I try to drop
> Twenty years eating figs in the pantry . . .
>   where the children
> Get off the bus   where the new
> Scoutmaster lives

and he recalls that twenty years ago he was a pilot, a "technical-minded stranger with my hands" dropping 300-gallon tanks filled with napalm and gasoline on people, ruthlessly destroying houses and neighborhoods much like his own.

> It consumes them in a hot
> Body-flash, old age or menopause
> Of children, clings and burns . . .

The combination of memory and horror, cruelty and callousness, stirs the reader with the force of a moral catharsis.

The poem is preceded by two mottoes. The quotation from the German writer, Günter Eich, would read in English: "Think about this, that after the most devastating destructions, every man will prove that he is not the one to be blamed."

LOUIS SIMPSON

was born in 1923 in Jamaica, West Indies. Educated in Jamaican British schools, he took his Ph.D. from Columbia University and taught there as well as at the State University of New York at Stony Brook. His prose works include a novel, *Riverside Drive*, and a critical study of the rustic English poet James Hogg, called "the Ettrick Shepherd." His poetry received various awards; his fourth volume, *At the End of the Open Road*, won the Pulitzer Prize in 1964. It was followed by *Selected Poems* and *Adventures of the Letter I*. "These poems," wrote Julian Symons in *The Sunday Times*, "are elegies for a lost dream of civilization, pursued through an imagined Russia (where the poet's mother was born) into an imaginary innocent America that turns into the metropolitan wasteland where only the insensitive survive."

America is Simpson's troubled preoccupation; he considers it devotedly, dispassionately, disturbingly. In "Lines Written Near San Francisco," he considers the unfulfilled potentialities and meditates that "while we were waiting for the land / They'd finished it," and that

> Whitman was wrong about the People,
> But right about himself. The land is within.
> At the end of the open road we come to ourselves.

Rich in imagery and irony, Simpson's poems flow naturally with "the currents that move from within." Inner currents propel *Air with Armed Men*, an unfinished autobiography that ranges from a discovery of his Jewish blood to an appraisal of the journalistic, literary, and academic worlds through which he struggled.

"Things" (page 150) is a clear and coherent look at familiar things with new perception. Imagination and irony combine to present the emanation of an Oriental commenting on the poet's everyday background:

> Things which to us in the pure state are mysterious,
> Are your simplest articles of household use . . .
> Machines are the animals of the Americans.

"After Midnight" (page 152) derives its effect from its concision and dramatic understatement. A single image intensifies the setting:

> The dark streets are deserted.
> With only a drugstore glowing
> Softly, like a sleeping body.

The conclusion is a purposeful and provocative anticlimax.

"Mashkin Hill" (page 153) is a plaintive reminiscence of an earlier time and place (the imagined Russia where the poet's mother was born?) supplanted by an overmechanized, overindulgent civilization. "Mr. Simpson seems embarrassed by his blessings," wrote an anonymous critic in the London *Times Literary Supplement.* "He is almost ashamed to be sane, competent, free. He is also embarrassed by his fellow-countrymen, saddened by the false finale of the American idyll." It is the sanity and freedom that lifts the poetry beyond competence.

ANTHONY HECHT

was born in 1923 in New York City. After receiving his B.A. degree from Bard College and his M.A. degree from Columbia University, he taught at Kenyon College, Bard College, and the University of Rochester. Chosen as a Fellow of the American Academy at Rome, he was the recipient of many honors and awards, including those from the Guggenheim Foundation and the Ford Foundation. His first book, *A Summoning of Stones*, published in 1954, was followed more than a dozen years later by *The Hard Hours* which, containing some of the best of the preceding book, won the Pulitzer Prize in 1968. With John Hollander he edited *Jiggery-Pokery*, a compendium of double dactyls, a new and sprightly form of light verse.

At first it appeared that Hecht had cultivated many elegant styles so adeptly that he had no style of his own. The London *Times* found that *A Summoning of Stones* was "too elegant, too cavalier, for its own good . . . but the great merit of *The Hard Hours* is that now the debts are paid." A poet of diverse manners, Hecht is alternately witty and grave, fastidious and forceful. He can turn from the half-wistful, half-flippant "Samuel Sewall" to the serious contemplation of " 'It Out-Herods Herod' " and the tragic nobility of " 'More Light! More Light!' "

"Samuel Sewall" (page 154) is a poet's neat compression of factual material. Born in England in 1652 Samuel Sewall was brought to New England at the age of nine. After being graduated from Harvard, he studied for the ministry, but decided to forgo the demands of the pulpit, became a printer and, later, a jurist. He left a most delightful and valuable diary, a many-faceted picture of the political, cultural, and social life of his day. One of the lighter and more engaging passages concerns the wooing of Madam Winthrop, a courtship which was unsuccessful. Sewall, a widower of sixty-eight, did not despair. He married a more responsive woman and lived contentedly ten more years.

" 'It Out-Herods Herod. I Pray You, Avoid It' " (page 156) is a quotation from Hamlet's advice to the players, adjuring them not to "tear a passion to tatters." The poem begins casually, but, while the children watch their favorite television show, their father thinks of the world where "All frequencies are loud/with signals of despair," where "the wicked have grown strong/Their numbers mock at death." Yet it is the poet, the father ("Half God, half Santa Claus") who, somehow, must

make the world behave
And put an end to grief.

The childermas referred to in the last stanza was a day of mourning (December 28th) in memory of the children massacred by Herod—a further meaningful implication in the title.

" 'More Light! More Light!' " (page 158). It is said that these were the last words of the dying Goethe. The condemned man in the first stanza is not identified, but he might well be the sixteenth century Chidiok Tichborne who, imprisoned in the Tower, wrote a moving poem, "On the Eve of His Execution," the night before he was hanged. Beginning with the third stanza, the scene changes. The place is "outside a German wood," evidently Buchenwald—by a horrible irony near Weimar, home of Goethe, the protagonist of German liberalism—the concentration camp where thousands of Jews were buried alive or thrown into gas ovens. The episode of the Pole who refused to dig living Jews into the grave actually happened.

W. D. SNODGRASS

was born in 1926 in Wilkinsburg, Pennsylvania, but the family moved to Beaver Falls, Pennsylvania, where he attended Geneva College. A year later he joined the Navy and, after his discharge, went to Iowa State College and concentrated on Renaissance literature. Attaining his master's degree, he moved about the country, teaching at Cornell University, Wayne State University in Detroit, the University of Rochester, and Syracuse University.

His first book, *Heart's Needle* (the title is taken from an Irish saying, "An only daughter is the needle of the heart") received the Pulitzer Prize. Largely autobiographical, it concerned Navy recollections, psychiatrist sessions, academic maladjustments, an unsuccessful marriage, and particularly, as evidenced by the title, the delicate relations with his young daughter. His second book, *After Experience*, continued the confessional mode—he and Robert Lowell were considered preeminent among those who wrote in this vein—a mode in which the psyche exposes and expresses itself. Unlike some of his contemporaries, Snodgrass does not indulge in either self-flagellation or self-pity; on the contrary, he presents his painful and sometimes absurd encounters with restraint and dignity. *After Experience* also includes luminous transmutations of paintings by Matisse, Manet, Monet, and Van

Gogh, as well as translations from Gerard de Nerval, Bonnefoy, Rimbaud, and Rilke, renderings that are enriched with the poet's own idiom.

"April Inventory" (page 160) is a half-sad, half-mocking portrait of the poet as teacher. It is colloquial and fresh, full of odd figures of speech: "The pear tree lets its petals drop/Like dandruff on a tabletop," "While scholars speak authority/And wear their ulcers on their sleeves," "Though trees turn bare and girls turn wives." The conclusion is both wry and whimsical:

> There is a loveliness exists,
> Preserves us, not for specialists.

"Mementos, 1" (page 163) is one of Snodgrass's divorce poems. Tactful and honest, it recalls a life shared "before we drained out one another's force/With lies, self-denial, unspoken regret/And the sick eyes that blame." It brings back a time when "needs were different" and "ideals came easy," a time that is gone, leaving only reminders, scattered mementos, a forgotten photograph. Here again Snodgrass summons remarkable images. For example:

> Like a man raking piles of dead leaves in his yard
> Who has turned up a severed hand.

"What We Said" (page 164) is an unhappy reminiscence of a couple's first estrangement and a pathetic determination (or hope) that, in a ruinous world, their love will survive the wreckage. The images are startling yet surprisingly apposite. The very setting reflects the lovers' apprehension. Leaves are "inflamed," "sick as words"; a discarded couch, "snarled in veins/Spilled its soiled, gray innards/Into a garbage mound"; a cluttered hole in the ground closes up "like a wound." The hurt self only implies the sense of loss and desolation; the poet lets the landscape say it for him.

ALLEN GINSBERG

son of a poet and teacher, was born in 1926, in Paterson, New Jersey. After attending Columbia University, he struck out for himself. He worked as a dishwasher, a book reviewer, a reporter for a labor newspaper. He traveled widely, to Paris, to Tangiers, to the Orient; his *Indian Journals* record the hopes and frustrations of efforts to find the essential self.

Ginsberg began as an outstanding member of the Beat Generation, a loose group that challenged literary values and exposed social disorders in the 1950s; it included such poets as Lawrence Ferlinghetti, Gary Snyder, Gregory Corso, and Robert Duncan. The Beats issued counterblasts to all that seemed stolid; they voiced an almost manic defiance of everything that represented the Establishment. Marijuana, reinforced by LSD and other drugs, helped demolish the proprieties; the Beats definitely were dedicated to beating things down.

It did not take long for Ginsberg to discover his own particular life style. His utterance was as exciting as it was energetic, often echoing a Whitmaniacal egocentricity, sometimes confused but always stubborn and courageous. It found fulfillment in *Howl*, which, violent and powerful, created a sensation when it appeared. It begins:

I saw the best minds of my generation destroyed by madness,
starving hysterical naked,

dragging themselves through the negro streets at dawn
looking for an angry fix,
angelheaded hipsters burning for the ancient heavenly
connection to the starry dynamo in the machinery of night.

This jeremiad against all the national shortcomings, a kind of angry instant poetry, did not become the pattern for Ginsberg's subsequent work. On the contrary, *Howl* was followed by *Kaddish*, an elegy written in memory of Ginsberg's mother. It is his longest as well as his best poem; according to Bruce Cook's *The Beat Generation*, it is "the finest single literary work to come out of the Beat movement."

"Kaddish" (page 166) is a ruthless, painful evocation of Ginsberg's paranoiac mother. The Hebrew word *Kaddish* denotes a praise of God and a prayer for the dead. In this instance it is an anguished reminiscence and a prolonged mourning. A schoolteacher devoted to radical causes, Naomi Ginsberg suffered a series of nervous breakdowns, sobbed and shouted that her husband was trying to kill her, that the hospital poisoned her food and put three big sticks down her back, that the radio was full of threatening voices. (In February, 1972, the poem was staged as a theater-video work and was highly praised.) Ginsberg's mother died a few years before what he called his "hymn, lament, litany, and fugue" was written.

"A Supermarket in California" (page 169) is obviously indebted to Whitman to whom the poem is addressed. The spirit of the "lonely old courage-teacher" is evoked with affection, adoration, and an incongruous but successful mixture of mysticism and humor.

W. S. MERWIN

was born in 1927 in New York City and grew up in New Jersey and Pennsylvania. Son of a Presbyterian minister, he majored in Romance languages at Princeton, went abroad and for twelve years worked as a tutor in Latin, French, Spanish, and Portuguese. It was in England that he established himself as a poet and also as translator of *The Song of Roland*, *The Satires of Persius*, *Spanish Ballads*, the epical *Poem of the Cid*, and *Selected Translations*, for which he received the P.E.N. Translation Prize in 1968.

Merwin's books of poetry have all borne provocative titles: *A Mask for Janus*, *The Dancing Bears*, *Green with Beasts*, *The Drunk in the Furnace*, *The Moving Target*, *The Lice*, and *The Carrier of Ladders*, which received the Pulitzer Prize in 1971. He declined to accept the prize money, declaring that "after years of the news from Southeast Asia and the commentary from Washington, I am too conscious of being an American to accept public congratulation with good grace, or to welcome it except as an occasion for expressing openly a shame which many Americans feel, day after day, helplessly and in silence."

As poet Merwin made a slow but discernible progress from tight metrical structures to relaxed open forms. *The Drunk in the Furnace*, for example, glows with warmth, an immediacy communicated in the autobiographical pictures of his family and in the easy flow of the title poem. The award-winning *The Carrier of Ladders* is proof of Merwin's ability to combine wildness and reality.

"The Drunk in the Furnace" (page 171) is a startling departure from Merwin's previous style and subject matter. For one thing, it is less precious than much of his earlier work; for another thing, it is broadly comic without being cheaply funny. The concluding picture has a Breughel-like effectiveness:

> When the furnace wakes, though, all afternoon
> Their witless offspring flock like piped rats to its siren
> Crescendo, and agape on the crumbling ridge
>   Stand in a row and learn.

"Small Woman on Willow Street" (page 172) is compounded of pity and horror in equal proportions. A frightening portent—"a hand/Is sneaking the whole sky another way"—it is an unforgettable picture.

"Western Country" (page 173) voices something of the despair Merwin indicated in his letter refusing the Pulitzer Prize. Bleakly he regards the cold landscape where "my countrymen are more cruel than their stars," and where each man moves with his gun.

GALWAY KINNELL

was born in 1927 in Providence, Rhode Island. Educated at Princeton University and the University of Rochester, he taught at various institutions including Chicago, Grenoble, and the University of Teheran in Iran. Poet-in-residence at several colleges, he translated medieval and contemporary French poetry and is the author of a novel, *Black Light*.

Kinnell's volumes of poetry—his fourth, *The Book of Nightmares*, was published in 1971—brim with controlled understated torments, impassioned poems about animals, and pity for the mortality of flesh. Kinnell is outraged about man's inhumanity to man and echoes Burns who also said that man was born to mourn. But although many of his poems deal with a depressive view of life, they leave the reader, as M. L. Rosenthal concluded in a review, "with something splendid: a true voice, a true song, memorably human."

"The Bear" (page 174) is a tour de force in every sense. It is a physical-psychical poem, a dream shaken by terror, a love-hate sharing, in which poet and bear are one. The ending of the poem, wrote Thomas Lask, "is less a surprise than a fulfillment."

"Vapor Trail Reflected in the Frog Pond" (page 178) is a poem in which Kinnell barely restrains his rage. The sound of a bomber cruising "in immaculate ozone" prompts him to quote Whitman with the most withering irony:

And I hear
coming over the hills, America singing,
her varied carols I hear:

What he hears is the "crack of deputies' rifles practicing their aim," the "sput of cattleprod," and

curses of the soldier as he poisons, burns, grinds, and stabs
the rice of the world,
with open mouth, crying strong, hysterical curses.

The sounds—the rifle shots, the cries and curses—inevitably lead the poet to what happened along the rice paddies of Asia, the horror that should never have occurred but which must be felt, faced—and somehow erased.

JOHN ASHBERY

was born in 1927 in Rochester, New York, was graduated from Harvard University and did advanced work at Columbia University, specializing in French literature. He spent ten years in Paris as a critic of modern art and became executive editor of *Art News*.

A leading member of "The New York School," his poetry is obviously indebted to the kind of painting he admired, especially the visual effects of the Surrealists. Ashbery's second book, *Some Trees*, was published as part of the Yale Series of Younger Poets and was introduced by W. H. Auden, who said that "from Rimbaud down to Mr. Ashbery, an important school of modern poets has been concerned with the discovery that, in childhood largely, in dreams and daydreams entirely, the imaginative life of the human individual stubbornly continues to live by the old magical notions."

Ashbery reflects "magical notions" in strange metaphors, distorted prosody, and a purposefully discontinuous syntax. It was objected that his "inconclusive verse" seemed like "an exercise in defining a void, like the efforts of modern engineering to achieve a complete vacuum." But Ashbery did not descend to controversy. He was aware that he was experimenting in a kind of poetry that departed from accepted norms. "I attempt to use words abstractly," he wrote, "as an abstract painter would use paint. . . .

My aim is to give meaning free play and the fullest possible range. As with the abstract painters, my abstraction is an attempt to get a greater, more complete kind of realism." At the same time, Ashbery did not repudiate the accommodating techniques of certain old established forms, as evidenced by his "Pantoum" and the intricate sestinas, "Faust" and "The Painter."

"Some Trees" (page 180) is, in spite of occasional dislocations, anything but a baffling poem. The rhymes and half-rhymes make a wavering music, and the images are fascinating—"as though speech / Were a still performance" . . . "A canvas on which emerges / A chorus of smiles." The interplay of meaning and suggestion is brilliant.

"The Painter" (page 181) is a poem cast in the shape of a sestina, that complicated form composed of six stanzas of six lines each, the lines of each stanza ending with the end words of the preceding stanza repeated in varying order. To make things more difficult, there is a final stanza of three lines in which all six end words of the preceding stanzas must be used. As a technical problem Ashbery overcomes all difficulties so adeptly that the reader is scarcely conscious of the skill involved. As a portrait, the subject is delineated not only with exactness but also with a refreshing, rippling humor, and the poem builds lightheartedly to its extravagantly fantastic finale.

JAMES WRIGHT

son of a factory worker, was born in 1927 in Martins Ferry, Ohio, studied at Kenyon College, in Vienna as a Fulbright Scholar, and at the University of Washington, from which he received his Ph.D. He taught at the University of Minnesota and at Hunter College and received a grant for creative work from the National Institute of Arts and Letters. In 1972 his poetry and his translations were awarded a prize of ten thousand dollars by the Academy of American Poets.

Although Wright's style has changed—his early work was traditionally formal—his central concern has always been with the sufferers, the stricken, the lonely ones—"I speak of flat defeat / In a flat voice." In *The Green Wall* he acknowledged his debt to Robert Frost and Edwin Arlington Robinson; but in the later volumes, *The Branch Will Not Break*, *Shall We Gather by the River*, and particularly in the *Collected Poems* which received the Pulitzer Prize in 1972, Wright's own voice comes through with a peculiar intensity. It is an intensity of compassion, a sharing, a love for animals and an empathy with the outcast.

"A Blessing" (page 183) is characteristic of Wright's feeling about natural things. The emanation of two ponies who come out of the willows to greet the poet and his friend is clearly delineative but it is also imaginative. "They ripple tensely, they can hardly contain their happiness. . . . They bow shyly as wet swans . . ."

The poet, enriched by the casual occurrence, is fulfilled beyond self.

> Suddenly I realize
> That if I stepped out of my body I would break
> Into blossom.

"Beginning" (page 184) is a further visionary sharing. The opening lines keynote the mood:

> The moon drops one or two feathers into the field.
> The dark wheat listens.

The grave whimsicality is sustained and deepened with "the moon's young, trying / Their wings" and the slender woman who "lifts up the lovely shadow / Of her face," "steps into the air" and is gone, while

> The wheat leans back toward its own darkness,
> And I lean toward mine.

"Mary Bly" (page 185) distills the pure substance of poetry in a few simple statements and suggestive images. One does not quickly forget the delicate hands "braiding the waters of air" and the colts cantering "without making a sound."

ANNE SEXTON

was born in 1928 in Newton, Massachusetts, attended private and public schools, and eloped at the age of nineteen. In her twenties she worked in the double role of librarian and fashion model, then settled in Weston with her husband and two daughters.

Although she had written many verses in high school, she did not attempt poetry again until she was in her late twenties when she studied with Robert Lowell and was awarded the Robert Frost Fellowship at the Bread Loaf Writers' Conference. She was one of the first Scholars at the Radcliffe Institute for Independent Study, the first traveling Fellow of the Academy of Arts and Letters, and was elected a Fellow of the Royal Society of Literature in London.

The title of her first volume, *To Bedlam and Part Way Back*, gives a key to her manner: a confessional poetry sharpened by wit and self-mockery. The subject matter is mental disturbance and psychic distress, but it is treated with such calmness and clarity that it delights even while it disturbs. Subsequent volumes showed a continual increase in range; detached observation mingled with passionate attachment and a fancy that was both contemplative and perky. Her third book, *Live or Die*, a luminous and exciting collection, won the Pulitzer Prize in 1967. It was followed by *Love Poems*, a series of unequivocal, unashamed, self-tortured, self-derisive, and moving communications; and in 1971 by *Transformations*, highly personal and often perverse reappraisals of familiar fairy tales told with fierce delight and diablerie.

"You, Doctor Martin" (page 186) reveals a spirit so agitated that it has been pushed across the borders of sanity. The picture of the institution is quietly realistic but the images are both odd and terrifying. It is the painful accuracy that gives the poem its poignance.

"Her Kind" (page 188) is a poem that is memorable not only for its convincing fantasy but also for the simple, almost casual tone in which the kinships are established. The neatly spaced rhymes give the telling an added flourish, an air of determined defiance.

"To a Friend Whose Work Has Come to Triumph" (page 189) has an interesting relationship. The title is a complement and contrast to a poem by William Butler Yeats, "To a Friend Whose Work Has Come to Nothing." The subject is the Breughel painting "The Fall of Icarus" which Auden considered in "Musée des Beaux Arts" (see page 71), but the tone and treatment differ greatly. Anne Sexton's sonnet is ironic from first to last, from the confident flyer "pasting those sticky wings on" to the concluding shrug:

> Who cares that he fell back to the sea?
> See him acclaiming the sun and come plunging down
> while his sensible daddy goes straight into town.

"Angel of Clean Sheets" (page 190) is another instance of the poet's flexible use of the sonnet form. It is also another reminiscence of a harrowing experience in the institution with its barred windows and multiple locks, where the poet-patient

> lay in a chloral cave of drugs
> as old as a dog, as quiet as a skeleton.

THOM GUNN

was born in 1929 in Gravesend, England. Educated at Cambridge, he moved to the United States as a student and remained as a teacher, critic, anthologist and, preeminently, poet. It was obvious that the American scene tended to shape his style and also his subject matter. He employed the measured syllabic method featured by Marianne Moore (see page 243) as well as the steady beat of lightly controlled verse. "I find," he said, "that in syllabics I can more easily record the casual perception, whereas with metrical verse I very often become committed to a particular kind of emotion, a rather clenched kind of emotion."

"Black Jackets" (page 191) from *My Sad Captains* unites both of Gunn's methods. It is in metrical rhymed verse and it records "the casual perception" with taut emotion. The poem is built on a series of sharp and effective details: the young trucker dressed up "to suit the Sunday hangout," the other drinkers "concocting selves for their impervious kit," the recollection of his initiation, the tattoos on his shoulders, the group's name and the slogan "Born To Lose." The picture is compact and complete.

"The Monster" (page 193) is a new and dramatic treatment of the *Doppelgänger*, a man's eerie double. In it the poet dreams or imagines he is walking toward the house of a rejected lover, sees a pathetic figure "ugly with despair" and realizes that it is himself. Sadly, he concludes:

> What if I were within the house,
> Happier than the fact had been
> —Would he, then, still be gazing here,
> The man who never can get in?
>
> Or would I, leaving at the dawn
> A suppler love than he could guess,
> Find him awake on my small bed,
> Demanding still some bitterness?

ADRIENNE RICH

was born in 1929 in Baltimore, Maryland, attended school there, was graduated from Radcliffe College, and lived in Cambridge, Massachusetts, in Holland, and in New York.

Her first book, *A Change of World*, was published in the Yale Series of Younger Poets and was introduced by W. H. Auden, who spoke of her acute ear and "an intuitive grasp of much subtler and more difficult matters like proportion, consistency of diction and tone, and the matching of these with the subject in hand." Subsequent volumes—*The Diamond Cutters*, *Snapshots of a Daughter-in-law*, *Necessities of Life*, *The Will to Change*—confirmed Auden's estimate and reinforced it with precision and a wry sense of humor. A poet of protest (*The Will to Change* cries for a change of national policies, in the ghettos, in our complacency), she says, "We are living through a time that needs to be lived through us," and adds, in another poem, "A life I didn't choose / chose me."

Besides her urgent poetry, Adrienne Rich has translated significant poems from the Dutch, poems that are relevant to the times and her own sensitive, somber perceptions.

"Living in Sin" (page 195) is a plain statement with subtle overtones. Both lovers—the night's careless companion and the disillusioned, order-loving woman—are not only suggested but thoroughly revealed through an accumulation of plain objects and arresting images. "No dust upon the furniture of love. / Half heresy, to wish the taps less vocal, / the panes relieved of grime." "She woke sometimes to feel the daylight coming / like a relentless milkman up the stairs."

"Planetarium" (page 196) illustrates what a critic called Adrienne Rich's way of telling a story "now by lucidity and again by obscurity . . . Her passion is all for singling out, fixing things in the mind so that hopefully and eventually the gaps between the things may be crossed."

Frederick William Herschel was born in Hanover and was sent to England where he worked as an organist at Bath and became an important musical authority before he turned to the study of astronomy. Revisiting Hanover, he brought back his sister Caroline, who collaborated with him not only in enlarging knowledge of the solar system but also surveying the entire heavens with telescopes made by their own hands. Although she acted as her brother's assistant, Caroline undertook independent observations, discovered various comets and nebulae, and published a catalogue of stars. Tycho Brahe was a sixteenth century Danish astronomer whose work concerning a plan of the cosmos was published in Uranisborg. A pulsar is one of very short-period radio sources emanating from the galaxy.

DEREK WALCOTT

was born in 1930 in St. Lucia, Windward Islands, British West Indies, and published his first volume, *Poems*, at nineteen. Educated at the University of the West Indies, he became a journalist, a teacher, and an art critic in Trinidad. He has lived briefly in the United States and in England, where the British Broadcasting Corporation produced some of the plays published in his *Dream on Monkey Mountain*.

Walcott's *Selected Poems* included most of *In a Green Night*, which had been published when he was thirty, with the addition of new poems. His intense sensory awareness was immediately recognized; a critic in *The Sphere* declared that Walcott was "balanced and compassionate in spite of angry tension of race, stringing his words together in a rich but measured pattern with the wry sadness of a Caribbean Eliot." *The Gulf* (1971) showed an enlargement of Walcott's vision and a quickening of social responsiveness. *Another Life* (1972), his longest, most ambitious poem, over four thousand lines of verse, evokes scenes of his divided childhood with the resolution of maturity.

"A Letter from Brooklyn" (page 198) is a touching but unsentimental tribute. The style is both straightforward and allusive. It would be rewarding to read it in context with E. E. Cummings' "my father moved through dooms of love" (page 49) and Dylan Thomas' "Do Not Go Gentle into that Good night" (page 105).

"Coral" (page 200) is a poem which, precise in observation, is richly suggestive. Irregular in rhythm and subdued in sonority, it is an imaginative and daringly inventive love lyric.

TED HUGHES

was born in 1930 in Yorkshire, was educated at Cambridge, and served with the Royal Air Force as ground wireless mechanic during World War II. Located at an isolated radio station in Yorkshire, he said he had "nothing to do but read Shakespeare and watch the grass grow." He was married to Sylvia Plath, by whom he had two children, lived for a while in the United States, and won the First Publication Award of the Poetry Center of the YM-YWHA in New York.

The Hawk in the Rain, *Lupercal*, *Wodwo*, and *Crow* increasingly disclose what has been called Hughes' "bestiary side," (more acridly, his beastliness) his identification with animals, his dislike of human beings, and his fondness for fierce, often unrestrained turbulence. "The natural world is still Mr. Hughes' chosen and proper domain," wrote a critic in the London *Times Literary Supplement*, adding that his gifts "are of a contained physical energy, dramatic but limited by a narrow range of sympathies."

"Her Husband" (page 201) has the background of Hughes' early upbringing: the grim industrial countryside with its foul, soot-dispensing collieries. It is an ugly picture, brutal, primitive, fully articulated but almost voiceless.

"Pibroch" (page 202) is a proof of Hughes' empathy with the sorrows of the natural world—the sea crying "with its meaningless voice," the imprisoned stone, the rushing wind "able to mingle with nothing," the tree struggling "to make leaves"—a world where "nothing lets up or develops." The title prepares the reader for the tone of trouble and complaint, for the pibroch is a doleful piece of music played on the bagpipe. It consists of a theme with variations, usually dirgelike in character.

SYLVIA PLATH

was born in 1932 in Winthrop, Massachusetts, of mixed Austrian, German, and Polish ancestry. She attended Smith College, received a Fulbright Fellowship, and went on to Newnham College, Cambridge, where she met the poet Ted Hughes. They were married; she bore her husband two children. A rootless sufferer (there had been early breakdowns) she found no settled happiness in marriage or in herself. After two suicide attempts, separated from her husband, she took her own life. She was thirty-one years old at the time of her death.

Her poems—her first book, the *Colossus*, was published in her late twenties—were produced in anguished bursts of intensity, naked revelations of maladjustment and misery. "Her fate and her themes are hardly separate," wrote Elizabeth Hardwick, "and both are singularly terrible. Her work is brutal, like the smash of a fist. . . . In the last months of her life she was visited by an almost hallucinating creativity. . . . The creative visitation was not from heaven but from the hell of rage. Yet so powerful is the art that one feels an unsettling elation as one reads the lacerating lines."

Ariel, a collection of poems written during her last months, and the posthumously published *Crossing the Water*, are pitiful, often hateful, but heartbreaking. Angry, aggressive, and self-consuming, it is as if the poet were devoured by her own furies and frustrations. An early, almost wholly autobiographical novel, *The*

Bell Jar, originally published under a pseudonym, presents a personality on the verge of disintegration, a creative spirit who had the power of transforming the ordinary into the terrifying.

The Art of Sylvia Plath, a symposium of biographical memoirs, reviews, essays, and scholarly examinations, was edited by Charles Newman and published toward the end of 1970.

"The Applicant" (page 203) is built on an accumulation of scorn and savage images. It is harsh and hateful not only toward the woman "applicant" but also against the poet herself. Robert Lowell wrote that many, after reading Sylvia Plath's poetry, "will recoil from their first overawed shock, and painfully wonder why so much of it leaves them empty, evasive, and inarticulate. . . . But most of us will turn back."

"Morning Song" (page 205) is a mother's response to her waking child. Since Sylvia Plath is the mother, the poem is not a prettified piece of sentiment; it is tart as well as tender. Yet, in spite of the seeming disassociation—"I'm no more your mother / Than the cloud that distils a mirror to reflect its own slow / Effacement at the wind's hand"—the tenderness is there.

"Daddy" (page 206) is Sylvia Plath's most cruel as well as her most celebrated poem. It is by no means a true portrait of her German-Polish father who died after a long illness and who was not in any way implicated in the annihilation of Jews at Dachau, Auschwitz, and Belsen. But the poet transfers her pain to all sufferers; she identifies herself with all the Jews in Europe, and her anguish mounts in a long scream of abuse. She tortures herself with a glorification of violence:

> Every woman adores a Fascist,
> The boot in the face, the brute
> Brute heart of a brute like you.

The outrage goes beyond reason. Even strangers join in hatred against the false presentment of her father—"A man in black with a Meinkampf look"—and stamp on him. "You cannot read the poem," wrote Elizabeth Hardwick, "without shivering. It is done, completed, perfected. All the hatred in your own heart finds its evil unforgiving music there." ("a Meinkampf look" refers to *Mein Kampf*, which was Hitler's self-glorifying book.)

WENDELL BERRY

was born in 1934 in Louisville, Kentucky, and received his B.A. and M.A. degrees from the University of Kentucky. As a teacher and member of the community, he is deeply concerned with certain manifestations of national power. As a countryman, he is involved with the use and abuse of man's environment. As a poet, he writes with crisp directness, a straightforwardness that reveals the observer who is also a passionate participant.

Besides the poems in *The Broken Ground* and *Openings*, Berry is also the author of two novels, *Nathan Coulter* and *A Place on Earth*, as well as two collections of essays, *The Long-Legged Horse* and *A Continuous Harmony*, the latter written with the good sense of an organic farmer.

"My Great-Grandfather's Slaves" (page 209) is a poem that grows from a summoned imagination—"Deep in the back ways of my mind"—to a summoning of responsibility. Quietly but eloquently it ends:

> I know that freedom can only be given,
> and it is the gift to the giver
> from the one who receives.

I am owned by the blood of all of them
who ever were owned by my blood.
We cannot be free of each other.

"Dark with Power" (page 211) is another poem in which Berry is both quiet and compelling. Without raising his voice, he speaks of the pity and the horror of war. Pointedly referring to America's devastation of Southeast Asia, he sees his countrymen as destroyers who are also self-destroying.

Dark with power, we remain
the invaders of our land, leaving
deserts where forests were,
scars where there were hills.

It is a poem that has the hush of an elegy and the slow penetration of pathos.

LEROI JONES

was born in 1934 in Newark, New Jersey, studied briefly at the Newark branch of Rutgers University, and entered Howard University in Washington. After graduating as an English major he served in the Air Force as a weatherman and B-36 gunner. He lived for a while in Greenwich Village and Harlem, but settled in his native Newark, where he established a black cultural center, adopted the name of Imamu Amiri Baraka, and was considered America's most prominent Negro literary figure as well as a political force.

His publications include two books of poetry which were highly praised; several successful plays, including the prize-winning *The Dutchman*; a novel, *The System of Dante's Hell*; a collection of short stories; a wide-ranging exposition of black music entitled *The Blues People*; two volumes of essays, *In Our Terribleness* and *Raise Race Rays Raze*. "As for black literature," he said, "it must function to bring us to an awareness that we are who we are—a weak, powerless, enslaved people—or it must give us the energy or the spirit to do something about our situation." In an effort to stir up his own people, Jones-Baraka, according to Alfred Kazin, "fuses poetry with prose, politics with religion, symbolism with invective."

"Leroy" (page 212) is obviously autobiographical. A reminiscence of the time when the "vantage of knowledge" passed on to his mother was passed on to him, it begins in nostalgia and ends in defiant determination.

"For Hettie" (page 213) is one of Jones's rare light-hearted moments. In an assumed gruff voice, he jokes insistently, divertingly and, by implication, tenderly about his left-handed wife.

JIM HARRISON

was born in 1939 in Northern Michigan where, like the poet Theodore Roethke, he learned to share the world of plant and animal life. A National Endowment of the Arts Fellowship and a Guggenheim Fellowship aided him to complete three volumes of poetry: *Plain Song*, *Locations*, and *Outlyer*. These were followed by a novel, *Wolf*, described by Jonathan Yardley as "raunchy, funny, swaggering, angry, cocksure, but also a handsomely written self-exploration."

As a poet, Harrison is plain-spoken and precise, with an innate empathy for everything that is alive and vulnerable. He presents a paradox: the solitary man who makes immediate and understanding contact with the commonest and most insignificant object encountered; a factual man who luxuriates in fantasies.

"Drinking Song" (page 214) is an unashamed acknowledgment of defeat or, if not defeat, a desire to escape thinking about a time when he could no longer hold his girl and when all his poems were born dead. It is a not altogether happy swagger that makes him say:

> I want to die in the saddle. An enemy of civilization.
> I want to walk around in the woods, fish and drink.

"Awake" (215) opens with the poet, a prey to insomnia, "limp with night fears," remembering how other poets, particularly Christopher Marlowe, died. Unable to sleep, he belabors himself—"I'm a bad poet broke and broken at thirty-two"—and tortures his mind with exaggerated fears, the recall of actual accidents, and sexual anxieties. Suddenly the poem leaps to its end with a most surprising and vivid metaphor:

> my soul, my heart, my brain
> my life so interminably struck with an ax
> as wet wood splits bluntly, mauled into
> sections for burning.

was born in 1942 in New York City. Of Russian-Polish-Jewish descent, she was educated at Barnard College and Columbia University Graduate School, where she received her M.A. for a study of Alexander Pope and bawdy eighteenth century poetry. During her early twenties she lived in Europe, taught English and writing at the University of Maryland's Overseas Divison in Heidelberg and, upon her return, continued to teach and give readings at various institutions throughout the country.

Her first volume, *Fruits & Vegetables*, is characterized by a captivating candor and impulsive spontaneity. Her vocabulary is fresh and all-inclusive. She uses eroticism as unaffectedly and as freely as any poet might use realism or romanticism. There is a clear sense of wholeness about her work, an appetite for every phase and feature of life, disdaining nothing. The poems are alternately (and often in the same poem) vivacious, ironic, fanciful—she pictures an old poet "with his face full of lines / with iambs jumping in his hair like fleas"—rueful, ribald, and always unabashed in their intimacy with the reader. Somehow she manages a blend of food and sex, cooking and the preparation of poetry. In the punningly mocking "Arse Poetica" she writes:

> Roast for an hour & twenty minutes, regulating
> heat so that the poem is always making quiet cooking

> noises. The poem is done when drumsticks move in
> their sockets & the last drops of juice drained from
> the vent run clear. Remove to a serving dish &
> discard trussing.

"The Teacher" (page 216) is typical of the boldness with which Erica Jong mixes reality and fantasy. An impish wit plays haphazardly through the lines. When the teacher walks, "sonnets divide / into octaves & sestets. / Couplets fall into place / when her fingers nervously toy / with the chalk." The students who once "might have taken life / by the scruff of its neck / in a neat couplet," now demand reality, "they need blood." The teacher is absorbed by those she has taught, and the poet wryly suggests:

> Eat this poem.

"The Quarrel" (page 218) achieves its effect of unhappy division with a sweep of unforeseen images: "when the wind beats at your door / like a man you have turned away" . . . "Your loneliness / is a small gray hole in the rain." The sense of futility closes in as

> You rise & go knocking
> at his locked front door.

"The Eggplant Epithalamion" (page 219). An epithalamion is part of an ancient ritual, a nuptial song celebrating the rites of love. In this poem the author wittily quotes the much-publicized archeologist Iris Love to prove that the eggplant is a love-inciting food. That the purple vegetable (aubergine in French) is actually an aphrodisiac is doubtful. But it is pleasant to think of the hundreds of poems it may have produced and the many who have fallen in love over an eggplant

> & have rocked to sleep
> in love's dark purple boat.

INDEX
of Titles and Authors

INDEX
of First Lines